How to Save a Failing Project
Chaos to Control

How to Save a Failing Project

Chaos to Control

Ralph R. Young, DBA

Steven M. Brady, PMP

Dennis C. Nagle, Jr.

MANAGEMENTCONCEPTS

ιιι
MANAGEMENTCONCEPTS
8230 Leesburg Pike, Suite 800
Vienna, VA 22182
(703) 790-9595
Fax: (703) 790-1371
www.managementconcepts.com

Printed in the United States of America

Library of Congress Cataloging-in-Publication Data

Young, Ralph Rowland.
   How to save a failing project : chaos to control / Ralph R. Young, Steven M. Brady,
   Dennis C. Nagle, Jr.
      p. cm.
   ISBN 978-1-56726-239-1
1. Project management. 2. Success in business. I. Brady, Steven M. II. Nagle,
Dennis C. III. Title.
HD69.P75Y65 2009
658.4'04—dc22

                                                                2008054770

10   9   8   7   6   5   4   3   2   1

Praise for *How to Save a Failing Project: Chaos to Control*

To Judy, who has enriched my life beyond my dreams!
To our amazing children, Kimberly, Jeff, and Matt,
who have given our lives meaning and fun! And to our
grandchildren, Madysen, Colin, Grace, Jonas, Michala,
and Caleb—our wishes for you: Follow your dreams!
Do what you love! Embrace life! Be a friend to all!
Be happy!

— RALPH YOUNG

To my wife of over 20 years, Robin . . . I never tell you
I love you enough. To my kids, Rachel and
Matthew . . . You are the lights of my life. Robin and
my kids bless my life on a daily basis and by
dedicating this book to you, I hope that in some small
way, you see how much I love and appreciate you.

— STEVEN BRADY

To my wife, Tanya, and sons, Lucas, Landon, and
Logan, you are my inspiration and greatest
supporters. To my Dad, thanks for always being there.

— DENNIS NAGLE

About the Authors

Ralph Young, DBA, has focused his career on managing and improving technical efforts, projects, and organizations. He has led projects and teams in different venues, including local and federal government, management information systems, systems and software engineering, process improvement, systems integration, and organizational change management. He has authored four books that address aspects of requirements engineering: *Effective Requirements Practices* (which explains *what* to do on a project and in an organization); *The Requirements Engineering Handbook* (which addresses *how* to perform requirements engineering); *Project Requirements: A Guide to Best Practices* (which recommends a set of best practices and explains *why* project managers should invest in the requirements process); and, with Paul J. Solomon, PMP, *Performance-Based Earned Value* (which proposes changing industry practices regarding the use of earned value techniques on a project to a performance-based approach). Dr. Young believes that leadership and effective requirements development and management are key factors in achieving successful project outcomes. He holds a BA in economics from the University of New Hampshire and an MA in economics and a DBA from The George Washington University.

Steve Brady, MBA, PMP, is a senior project manager with more than 14 years of project management experience. His professional experience includes some 20 years in the information technology industry, providing project management, organizational process development, and strategic planning. As a project manager, Mr. Brady has led both custom software development and commercial off-the-shelf (COTS) product implementations. He is versed in every area of the development life cycle and has led projects for federal, state, and local governments. Throughout his career, Mr. Brady has developed and executed organizational processes in a number of firms, including Motorola, Northrop Grumman, and TASC Inc. He specializes in executing projects using mature processes and has five years of experience leading a Capability Maturity Model® Integration (CMMI) Level 5 project, the Software Engineering Institute's highest maturity level. He holds a BS in management of information systems and an MBA from Wright State University.

Dennis Nagle, Jr., has spent more than 20 years as an engineer on many project teams, both as a programmer and also the principal software architect. Based on this experience, he brings the developer's or performer's point of view to the project management process. Mr. Nagle is certified in the Personal Software Process (PSP) as defined by the Software Engineering Institute at Carnegie Mellon University. He received a Northrop Grumman Achievement Award for his significant contribution toward his business unit's receiving a Capability Maturity Model® Integration (CMMI) Level 5 rating. Mr. Nagle believes that managing stakeholder expectations and creating accurate estimates based on historical data are crucial for successful projects. He holds a BS in computer science from Virginia Tech and an MS in computer science from Wright State University.

Contents

FIGURES

Foreword

I have had the pleasure of knowing Ralph Young for many years now. He and his co-authors, Steve Brady and Dennis Nagle, are especially well qualified to write about one of the key practical issues in systems and software development: how to manage a successful project.

Fundamentally, systems engineering is simple: you find out what the client wants; you work out how to meet that need; and you implement the resulting specifications. The project management component is equally straightforward: you plan according to the client's need, and you monitor and control the implementation of the plan. The authors of this admirably clear and practical book present well-established techniques for managing a successful project. These techniques do not amount to rocket science, though they are as suitable for developing satellite launchers as for any other complex hardware or software.

The authors note in the Introduction the prevalence of project failures repeated year after year. Critical project management tools and techniques are not sinking in, despite the wide array of available resources. People go on believing that they can buck the trend—that the rules do not apply to them. There is something joyously human in the self-confidence and optimism of engineers and project managers alike: this time we can make it! Can we fix it? Yes we can! Energy and enthusiasm are admirable and necessary to successful projects—but factors such as poorly defined requirements, creeping scope, conflicting and unmanaged expectations, and a lack of control can bring disaster to any project. The authors wisely emphasize these key points right up front in this book.

Success depends on teamwork: on a common purpose, on agreed-upon goals, and on people in different roles working effectively together. Many engineering textbooks barely mention project management; many project management books barely consider engineering. Young and his team are as comfortable quoting software and systems engineers as they are project management gurus. They draw pragmatically on six sigma, requirements engineering, software estimation, systems engineering, peer review, software inspection, earned value, and many other concepts and techniques.

How to Save a Failing Project takes an honest look at some of the uncomfortable topics in project management we all know but prefer not to speak about, such as the signs—both overt and subtle—that a project is out of control.

The book also shows how to save troubled projects by applying leadership, planning, communication, and effective processes, and by building and maintaining a good team of people, using metrics, learning from mistakes, and taking action to implement those lessons. These components are well documented and are easily learned. Applying metrics, for example, can help project managers predict with mathematical precision how many defects will occur during a project, allowing them to plan for those defects.

If you're reading this book in a time of project crisis, be reassured that this book offers a wealth of project experience and calm, practical, step-by-step guidance. The authors have seen many projects in crisis, and they have turned many of them around. I hope very much that you will come to appreciate their wisdom and value the crucial importance of good requirements—and requirements analysts—in establishing and planning projects properly.

If you're reading this book in between projects, Part III offers guidance on how to improve your chances for project success the next time around. Again, the techniques offered are not quantum mechanics, but simple things like defining many small milestones can make both project progress and deviations from the plan easy to identify.

We need to be reminded how central and critical the basics of requirements work—discovering stakeholders' goals and expectations, identifying and agreeing on scope, evolving the real requirements, and prioritizing, tracing, and managing changes to requirements—are to project success. These are not minor technical matters to leave to junior engineers in a quiet backwater of your project. These things determine the project's success or failure more directly than anything else.

Ian Alexander
February 2009
www.scenarioplus.org.uk

Preface

Poor project results are all too common. We often hear about projects that are canceled, go over budget, are completed late, or deliver less functionality than promised. Customers are dissatisfied, users are disappointed, and project staff are frustrated and overworked. Program and project managers may even lose their jobs.

Completing projects successfully is difficult. Projects involve people, goals, objectives, expectations, budgets, schedules, deliverables, and deadlines. It's hard to keep everything on track. It's especially difficult to realize in advance that a project is getting off track. The later in the project process, the more challenging it is to get back on course. Our goal is to arm you with tools and techniques that will help you deal with some of these difficulties.

This book will help you:

- Understand the value of developing a project plan (that is, planning before acting)

- Use and continuously update your project plan as you execute your project

- Recognize signs that your project is deviating from the approach needed for successful completion

- Develop a set of measures that provide insight into the health of your project

- Identify and implement steps to get your project back on track
- Avoid getting into trouble on future projects.

The inspiration for this book came when we were called into action to turn around a failing project. We were struck by the lack of practical information available to the team on how to apply actions that would turn the project around. To that end, in this book we share our experience and provide the methods, techniques, and tools you need to save a failing project and also to keep your project from getting into trouble in the first place. We then recommend an approach that will enable all members of your project team to embrace a mindset of continuous improvement.

This book is organized into three parts. Part I, Project Awareness, addresses the typical reasons that projects fail, ways to recognize a project headed for failure, and the end results of a failed project. Part II, Project Planning, focuses on how to end the chaos. We address the following topics:

- Defining project goals and objectives
- Developing a plan to produce a realistic project plan
- Building a team
- Identifying the project's products
- Identifying and estimating the work required to produce the needed products
- Developing a viable schedule
- Creating the actual planning document.

Part III, Project Execution, explains how to keep the project moving toward successful completion. We offer techniques to help you:

- Execute your plan
- Communicate and manage stakeholder expectations
- Manage project scope

- Maintain product quality

- Optimize project performance through refinement of the plan.

This is not rocket science. This is common sense. We know (or can find out) what we need to do. Ours is the responsibility to do what needs to be done to ensure that our projects are successful, our customers are satisfied, our users' real needs are met, our companies enjoy a reasonable profit, and our project team members are fulfilled by their work assignments.

We wrote this book with the intent of giving you the knowledge, insight, and tools you need to recognize that a project is in trouble, determine what to do about it, transform a failing project into a successful one, and keep from getting into difficulty on future projects. We hope that your time spent with this book will be valuable and trust that you will find the guidance, information, and encouragement you seek.

And finally, we the authors have a sincere request of you, the reader. We would appreciate reader feedback and data, if available, regarding the impact that the processes, suggestions, and recommended approaches provided in this book have had on your projects. This information will guide subsequent editions of this book and other publications that will continue to help readers plan and execute successful projects in the future. Please email your feedback to Ralph Young at ryoungrr@aol.com. In return, look for helpful advice and useful downloadable artifacts at www.ralphyoung.net.

Ralph Young
Steve Brady
Dennis Nagle
February 2009

Acknowledgments

We would like to acknowledge all the team members we have worked with and learned from in the past. Their work has enabled us to put the concepts in this book into practice. We would also like to thank Myra Strauss, Courtney Chiaparas, and Jill Sulam for transforming our concepts and rough paragraphs into a real book.

Dennis would like to thank Gabe Hoffman, Sherri Turner, and Bryan Thurston for their counsel.

Steve would like to personally acknowledge the Inventory Tracking System team, who came as close to perfecting these concepts as any team could hope to, and Hal Miller, who taught him how science and statistical process control can be applied to the art of software development.

Ralph would like to offer special thanks to Rich Raphael for his enthusiastic and helpful support over many years and to Doug Woods for his suggestions regarding reader feedback.

Finally, we would like to thank our families and friends for encouragement and support.

Introduction

A successful project can be defined as one that is completed within a set budget and schedule and that meets identified goals and objectives. But if project success can be defined in one sentence, why do so many projects fail? Projects fail for a number of reasons, including:

- Unachievable objectives

- Unreasonable expectations

- Inadequate planning

- Unclear requirements and ineffective requirements practices

- Ineffective communication

- Insufficient resources (often resulting from poor estimation of the work required to conduct the project)

- Ineffective project tracking capabilities

- Poor quality and insufficient quality control.[1]

It is disheartening to study analyses of U.S. Department of Defense (DOD) projects that have struggled or failed. These reviews, conducted by various bodies over a long period of time, have come to similar conclusions about the root causes of the problems and what needs to be done about them.[2] Unfortunately, little has been done as a result of the studies and findings—the recommendations simply have not been implemented.

We suspect that the situation is similar among non-DOD projects, as well as in Europe, Australia, India, and elsewhere.

How can you determine if your project is out of control? Indicators of an out-of-control project include missed milestones[3] and deliverables, differing opinions of the project's goals and objectives, exceeded budgets, missed schedules, dependence on heroes, customer dissatisfaction and disapproval, frustrated staff, and concerns voiced by various and many stakeholders. The frustration, hopelessness, and stress experienced by the project manager (PM) and others often leads to finger pointing. Most often the PM is blamed—and sometimes replaced.

Projects usually can be saved. The characteristics of successful projects are components of the strategy that can be used to save a failing project. These include:

- *Leadership.* The PM must step up to the challenge of saving the project by recognizing the situation, calling a halt to ineffective ongoing work activities, leading the effort to develop a viable plan (described in Part II, Project Planning), and then implementing the plan and replanning as necessary (described in Part III, Project Execution).

- *Planning.* A "collusion of optimists"[4] undermines the development of a viable project plan. Almost always, there is pressure to meet unreasonable and unrealistic project objectives. These objectives tend to be set based on arbitrary deadlines (such as the date of a trade show) rather than on any realistic estimate of what is required to get the job done. The project's stakeholders need our help and support to determine what is reasonably achievable. Try to negotiate with the stakeholders. You might deliver a portion of the project earlier, have multiple releases of products, or create different versions of the products needed. The PM and his or her project team must develop realistic estimates of the work products to be created and the tasks to be performed before establishing a project schedule. To do so, they'll create a product breakdown structure (PBS) and a work breakdown structure (WBS).

The estimates provided by developers are generally optimistic. This compounds project problems. Executives like optimistic estimates because they imply that desirable business targets are achievable. Managers like optimistic estimates because they suggest an ability to support upper management's objectives.[5] But when estimates to complete needed work are unrealistic and unachievable, the project is doomed to failure.

It is also important to differentiate between estimates and commitments. From experience, we know that our estimates are usually wrong; they are often 200 to 300 percent lower than they should be. Why do project teams so often underestimate how long it will take to perform tasks? In large part, underestimates stem from not accounting for all activities involved in developing a product, including receiving phone calls, reading e-mails, and attending administrative meetings. Therefore, it is crucial to obtain more information and consider past experiences before we make commitments. Note that estimates are most often stated as ranges, whereas a commitment is most often given as a point in time—which greatly increases the probability that the commitment will not be met by the target date.

■ *Communication.* Good communication during a fast-moving project is difficult. The PM must create proactive mechanisms to facilitate effective communication, including:

- Holding weekly meetings with the leads of all project areas to discuss developments

- Scheduling brown-bag sessions to keep the staff informed and to foster open communication

- Posting color-coded lists of action items in the hallways. "Red" items might inspire the person responsible to take immediate action.

- Requiring that minutes of meetings be taken and posted promptly

- ◆ Using rules of conduct to encourage positive interpersonal interaction

- ◆ Having and using guidelines for good meetings, such as inviting only those who really must attend.[6]

- **Defined processes.** The processes used for key activities such as project planning, project tracking, requirements development and management, configuration management, quality assurance, peer reviews, and defect prevention are often undocumented and are not continuously improved. Yet we wonder why we have chaos on projects! Having defined, documented processes and procedures significantly enhances productivity and increases the likelihood of project success.

- **Use of templates.** Reusing available templates, rather than starting anew on each project, is extremely helpful.

- **Qualified employees.** It should come as no surprise that qualified employees are necessary. The COCOMO II estimation model has shown that personnel factors significantly influence project outcomes. According to Steve McConnell, a requirements analyst's competency or lack thereof has a greater effect on project outcomes than does any other factor. His analysis indicates that a project ranking worst in each category of the model would require 22 times as much effort to succeed as would a project that ranked best in each category. (For more about the COCOMO II estimation model, see Resources and Suggested Reading at the end of the Introduction.)

- **Metrics.** Most projects make use of measures and metrics, but often the metrics used do not provide insight into the issues that must be addressed. Projects are most often measured based on cost, schedule, and the usefulness of the product. We recommend using forward-looking measures such as a Rayleigh curve, which predicts future defects based on proven mathematical equations.

- **Optimization.** Identifying lessons learned after each project phase is an easy way to improve your project. By identifying problems while the project is still being executed, your current project, rather than a future project, benefits. Conducting a defect-prevention cycle identifies problems based on objective data analysis rather than subjective opinions.

Which Processes and Practices Are Critical?

Realistic scheduling and project success depend on the successful integration of critical processes and practices that are supported by appropriate infrastructure and data collection activities. These include:

- *Project planning,* including identifying the work products and developing accurate estimates of product size and work errors required.

- *Project tracking,* including selecting and using appropriate measures, notably forward-looking measures.

- *Requirements development,* which includes eliciting the real requirements and investing in the requirements process. Your requirements analyst's capabilities, expertise, and experience will have a major effect on the project's success.

- *Requirements management,* particularly the use of an effective mechanism to control new requirements and changes to requirements. Of course, it is not possible to anticipate all requirements at the beginning of a project effort; thus, it is essential to plan methods of addressing new and changed requirements as they emerge.

- *Peer reviews and inspections,* so that errors and defects can be eliminated early in the development effort.

- *Defect prevention,* which addresses the problems on a project and develops, implements, and tracks countermeasures.

- *Risk management,* a process that can significantly and positively change a project. The PM should initiate the risk management process early, including the development of risk mitigation and contingency plans, and pay close attention to it throughout the project.[7]

In Brief

PMs, team members, and stakeholders can all influence the direction of a project. Applying just some of the recommended techniques presented in this book can benefit your project. By using the approach recommended in this book, you will produce higher-quality products, minimize rework, achieve cost/schedule predictability, satisfy customers, and fulfill staff. On a more personal level, you can take great satisfaction in providing the leadership and guidance to enable successful completion of an important effort.

Suggested Reading and Resources

COCOMO II. Constructive Cost Model II (COCOMO II) is a model that allows the user to estimate the cost, effort, and schedule when planning a new software development activity. COCOMO II is the latest major extension to the original COCOMO model published in 1981 (COCOMO 81). It consists of three sub-models, each offering increased fidelity the further along one is in the project planning and design process. These sub-models, listed in order of increased fidelity, are called the Applications Composition, Early Design, and Post-Architecture models.

COCOMO II can be used in situations such as:

- Making investment or other financial decisions involving a software development effort

- Setting project budgets and schedules as a basis for planning and control

- Deciding on or negotiating tradeoffs among software cost, schedule, functionality, performance, or quality factors

- Making risk management decisions about software cost and schedule

- Deciding which parts of a software system to develop, reuse, lease, or purchase

- Making decisions about legacy software inventory: what parts to modify, phase out, or outsource

- Setting mixed investment strategies to improve an organization's software capability via reuse, tools, process maturity, or outsourcing

- Deciding how to implement a process improvement strategy, such as the one provided in the Software Engineering Institute's Capability Maturity Model® Integration (CMMI).

For more information, go to http://sunset.usc.edu/csse/research/COCOMOII/cocomo_main.html.

Data & Analysis Center for Software (DACS) Gold Practices Website. The website provides information about prevalent software acquisition and development best practices that may reduce program risks and increase return on investment. Helpful pages include:

- Management and measurement: www.goldpractices.com/practices/mbs/index.php

- Requirements: www.goldpractices.com/practices/rto/index.php

Project Management Institute. *Guide to the Project Management Body of Knowledge (PMBOK® Guide),* **3rd ed. Newtown Square, PA: Project Management Institute, 2004.** This guide sets a widely recognized and endorsed standard for the project management industry. It provides a project management framework that specifies all the processes used to manage a project, categorized into nine knowledge areas: project integration management, project scope management, project time management, project cost management, project quality management, project human resource management, project communications management, project risk management, and project procurement management.

Wiegers, Karl E. *Practical Project Initiation.* **Redmond, WA: Microsoft Press, 2007.** Wiegers, who has many years of experience and valuable insights and suggestions, provides simple checklists and other tools readers can use to make the project initiation process more effective and efficient. Helpful icons denote true stories and also common project initiation traps to avoid.

Notes

1. Industry expert Capers Jones observes that effective software quality control is the most important single factor preventing project delays and disasters because finding and fixing bugs are the most expensive and the most time-intensive activities for large systems. ("Preventing Software Failure: Problems Noted in Breach of Contract Litigation," October 2008, p. 5.)

2. See, for example, the *Report of the Defense Science Board (DSB) Task Force on Defense Software,* November 2000 (www.acq.osd.mil/dsb/reports/defensesoftware.pdf). The Task Force reviewed six major DOD-wide studies that had been performed on software development and acquisition projects since 1987. They noted that these studies contained 134 recommendations, only a very few of which have been implemented.

3. Capers Jones notes that in litigation where he worked as an expert witness, milestones were very informal and consisted primarily of calendar dates. He recommends instead that milestones should be based on the validation of complete work activities (e.g., requirements document completed, cost tracking system initialized, functional specification completed). ("Preventing Software Failure: Problems Noted in Breach of Contract Litigation," October 2008, p. 10.)

4. Steve McConnell, *Software Estimation: Demystifying the Black Art* (Redmond, WA: Microsoft Press, 2006): 47.

5. Ibid.

6. See Table 7-1 in Ralph R. Young, *Project Requirements: A Guide to Best Practices* (Vienna, VA: Management Concepts, 2006) for a list of suggested communications aids for a project.

7. For an insightful and helpful discussion of managing project risk, see J. Steven Waddell, "Requirements, Risk, and the Project Manager," Chapter 11 in Young, *Project Requirements: A Guide to Best Practices* (169–186). Waddell provides a thorough discussion of the risk management process and risk response strategies PMs should use.

I

Project Awareness
How to Recognize a
Failing Project

1 Why Projects Fail

The data on project success rates are alarming. According to the Standish Group's CHAOS Report, based on biennial surveys of software project outcomes, about 75 percent of all software projects are delivered late or fail. The data also show that since 2002, the rate of successful project completion has dropped significantly.[1]

Delayed projects are not problematic simply because they are late. On a late project, significant planned functionality is often discarded in an effort to stay on schedule and keep costs down. So the average schedule overrun of about 120 percent and average cost overrun of 100 percent shown in Figure 1-1 are significantly understated. Completing projects often takes more than twice as long and costs twice as much as we estimate! How can it be that we haven't made progress in delivering software on time or under budget? In 1981, Barry Boehm provided a seven-step approach to estimating software projects in *Software Engineering Economics.* Yet most projects today do not use even this level of discipline in preparing estimates.

Steve McConnell, author of *Software Estimation: Demystifying the Black Art,* writes, "The industry data show that the software industry has an underestimation problem. Before we can make our estimates more accurate, we need to start making the estimates bigger. That is the key challenge for many organizations."[2] Industry expert Capers Jones writes that the root cause of project failure is poor project management, not technical issues or the competence and ability of technical personnel.[3]

FIGURE 1-1: Software Project Outcomes, 1994–2004

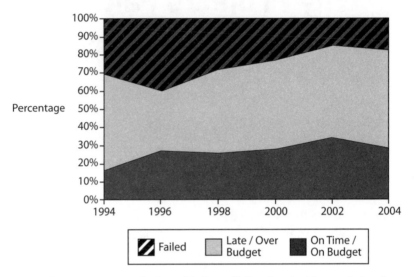

From *Software Estimation*, by Steve McConnell. Reprinted with permission from Microsoft Corporation.

The failure to adequately plan using useful and effective measures is the root cause of project failure. This book will enable you to save a failing project. Even better, it will enable you to manage projects while reducing the risk of failure.

Key Factors Leading to Failure

While many factors lead to the failure of a project, in the authors' experience, a few specific, easily recognizable factors signal serious problems that jeopardize project success:

- Poorly defined requirements
- Scope creep
- Stakeholders have different expectations
- Stakeholders have unrealistic expectations

- There is no real need or demand for the product
- There is a lack of user involvement in the project
- Change management is lacking or ineffective
- Poor quality control
- Problems are caught too late
- There is no project champion.[4]

Poorly Defined Requirements

Execution of the project is begun prematurely, before requirements are defined, analyzed, and agreed upon. The team then performs a great deal of technical work that lacks a focused vision of the real needs, objectives, and work products.

Scope Creep

New requirements and changes to requirements are accepted without any control or management of the requirements. This *scope creep* occurs on all projects and is one of the major reasons that projects get out of control. (Chapter 12 provides several suggestions for controlling scope creep.)

Stakeholders Have Different Expectations

A *stakeholder* is anyone who has an interest in the success or failure of a project. A critical basic foundation for successful project planning and execution is that all (or at least as many as possible) of the stakeholders need to be identified at the outset,[5] and their objectives and expectations must be stated, refined, and clarified.

Project stakeholders may include the customer, end users, customer management, developer's PM, developer's management team, corporate stockholders, project team members, subcontractors, and the contracts office.

Writing a vision and scope document is an effective way to facilitate the process of identifying, refining, and clarifying stakeholder needs and expectations.[6] This document should provide a vision for the project that is broad enough for all stakeholders to embrace, and it should clarify a reasonable scope (what is to be included or excluded). You'll learn more about the vision and scope document in Chapter 12.

Figure 1-2 delineates each type of stakeholder's expectations with regard to project success.

Managing these expectations is essential. Different stakeholder groups will have different needs and expectations. For example, *customers* may consider these factors when evaluating a project:

- Timely completion

- Completion within budget

FIGURE 1-2: What Must Happen for Stakeholders to Consider a Project Successful?

What Must Happen for Stakeholders to Consider a Project Successful?												
Category of stakeholders \ **Success factors/ criteria**	Timely completion	Completion within budget	Meeting agreed-upon requirements	Extent of functional requirements and features	Productive teaming or partnership approach	Profit realized	Follow-on business	Minimal overtime required	Appreciation and recognition	Challenging learning experience or technical growth	Being paid well	Quality	Fulfillment of terms and conditions of contract
Customer	X	X	X	X	X							X	
End user	X		X	X	X			X				X	
Customer management	X	X	X	X	X			X	X			X	
Developer project manager (PM)	X	X	X	X	X	X	X	X	X		X	X	X
Developer PM's management	X	X	X		X	X	X	X				X	X
Project team member	X		X		X		X	X	X	X	X	X	
Subcontractors	X	X			X	X	X	X	X		X	X	
Contracts office	X												X

- Project meets the agreed-upon requirements

- Whether a team/partnership approach was used to plan and execute the project.

Users may have a somewhat different perspective—they also are likely to be interested in timely completion of the project, but they may be more focused on the functional requirements and features of the delivered products, system, or software development effort than they are on completion within the allocated or planned budget.

It's important to realize that there may be several subcategories of users, and each subcategory may be primarily interested in a somewhat different set of functional capabilities. This is a major reason that the requirements elicitation methods and techniques you choose must provide a mechanism for prioritizing the requirements and helping each subcategory of users understand the vision, needs, and objectives of the other subcategory groups. (*Requirements elicitation* is the process of determining the real requirements. *Real requirements* are a subset of the stated requirements that are verifiable and prioritize needs for a particular system or capability.)[7]

The project *developer/supplier* is perhaps most interested in the team or partnership approach that is used to execute the project and in making a profit.

Project team members may be most concerned about their quality of life (read: they want to work minimal overtime). They want to do fulfilling work that is challenging and that offers technical growth and professional development, and they seek appreciation and recognition.

Subcontractors may be primarily interested in being paid well for their expertise and experience. And finally, the customer's and developer's *contracts officers* may be most focused on ensuring that the terms and conditions of the contract are met by the other party.

Project weaknesses or problems can cause stakeholder groups to have dissenting opinions. These problems can include:

- Failure to write a vision and scope document, to circulate it to the various stakeholder groups, and to reach agreement on what the project will accomplish.

- Failure to identify the *stated requirements* (the requirements provided by a customer at the beginning of a development effort) of the stakeholder groups and to work with them to reach some consensus on the real requirements for the project.[8]

- Failure to put in place an effective mechanism to control changes to requirements and limit new requirements, which will inevitably be discovered as the project proceeds.

- Failure to perform effective requirements analysis to gain insight into what is really required to deliver the desired work products and results. *Requirements analysis* is a structured, organized method of determining the product attributes that will satisfy a customer need.

- Failure to build in quality during the performance of the project. Quality products can be defined as those meeting real customer needs. How can your project team ensure quality?

  - *Perform peer reviews and inspections of the work products.* This is one of the most effective ways to discover problems, errors, defects, and omitted requirements. We have observed that peer reviews can detect approximately 75 percent of the defects in the reviewed product.

  - *Ensure testability* of each requirement at the beginning of the effort. This will save money and time during testing.

  - *Always use a defect prevention process,* regardless of the *process maturity level* of the project (the degree to which defined, documented, trained, and understood processes are used).

It's important to realize that the "success" or "failure" of a project is based on each particular stakeholder's perspective. Therefore, the effective program or project manager must tailor her or his communications to each stakeholder audience, keeping each group's needs in mind. Moreover, the PM must make a concerted, continual effort to keep each stakeholder group informed, engaged, and actively supporting the project.

Keep in mind that you may have negative stakeholders—those who hope (openly or secretly) that your program or project fails. Someone who fears having to learn new ways of performing work when your project replaces an old system might be a negative stakeholder. The PM must be sensitive to the possibility of negative stakeholders and ready to develop strategies to overcome resistance.

Stakeholders Have Unrealistic Expectations

Very often, customers and users have unrealistic expectations of what a project, system, or software development effort will do or address. Unless the project team clearly defines and communicates the results it anticipates, these stakeholders may assume that the project will fulfill all of their needs—even those that are unreasonable. You might try to appease stakeholders who have such expectations by sharing with them a plan to release products and updated versions of those products over a reasonable period of time.

There Is No Real Need or Demand for the Product

Developing a product for which there is no need or demand is a sure-fire way to lose money and render a project unsuccessful. The English Channel Tunnel, also known as the Chunnel, is one mega-project that is considered a failure. The Chunnel is a 31-mile rail tunnel connecting England and northern France beneath the English Channel. The developers thought that people would be willing to pay anything to be able to make a quicker trip between the two countries. In reality, however, many travelers prefer taking the ferry for the scenery and relaxation. The Chunnel is an economic failure due to lack of customer demand.

There Is a Lack of User Involvement in the Project

Projects that involve users extensively throughout the project life cycle are more successful. Figure 1-3 shows how the PM can involve users throughout the project.

Change Management Is Lacking or Ineffective

When developing products, it's essential to provide *configuration control,* or careful tracking of the work products, versions, and releases, so that everyone has access to the current material. It is all too easy for projects to spiral out of control because of ineffective change management.

Poor Quality Control

All work products must be subject to quality control through peer reviews and effective quality assurance procedures. Quality work products meet requirements and are free of defects. Having defect-removal

---

FIGURE 1-3: Involving Customers and Users in Your Project

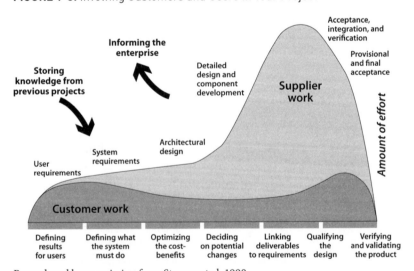

Reproduced by permission from Stevens et al. 1998.

processes in place is not enough. A quality assurance team must conduct process audits and analyze data to verify that these processes are being followed. Chapter 13 discusses quality control techniques in greater detail.

Problems Are Caught Too Late

Many project management books and articles recommend a set of measures (often called *metrics*) to help keep track of the work being performed on a project. Standard project metrics include headcount (the number of people assigned to the project), cost, quality, customer satisfaction, and schedule variance, to name just a few. The major problem with these metrics is that they are all *lagging indicators*—that is, they provide insight into what has already happened. As a result, a problem can become quite big before we even realize that we *have* a problem—and then we must figure out how to address it and implement the solution.

A related problem that often compounds the situation is that managers often want to hear only good news. If the project environment does not encourage trust, honesty,[9] and open communication, the project staff may not report problems, issues, or negative metrics. Management, then, does not learn about problems (potential or real) early enough to help the team handle them.

Arbitrary targets set by upper management are yet another problem. Senior managers often think that missing a target is unacceptable. It should be no surprise, then, that teams often report only what senior management expects to hear—that the targets have been met, even if they actually have not.

The result of our reliance on lagging indicators and of indulging these management expectations is that underlying problems and difficulties are not discovered or reported during the project performance period, when they could be fixed. Rather, we suddenly discover that the task, phase, or project is a gigantic failure at the end. We seem to prefer to hear very bad news at the end of a project rather than in smaller doses earlier on, when problems actually crop up.

The End Results of a Failed Project

Truly successful projects meet the needs of *all* stakeholders. When one stakeholder is unhappy, the project has failed that stakeholder to some extent. If enough stakeholders are unhappy for a long period of time, the project most likely will be terminated, and all stakeholders will be severely affected. It's very important to balance the needs and expectations of all stakeholders in order to execute a truly successful project.

Remember that a project's success or failure is based on stakeholders' perceptions. Take, for example, a project that produced an exceptional, high-quality product on time and within budget. The customer is ecstatic, and the company made a profit. But the team members worked 80 hours a week for months to complete the tasks. At the end of the project, they were exhausted, and some decided to leave the company. Was this really a successful project?

Truly successful projects meet the needs of all stakeholders. When one stakeholder is unhappy, the project has failed that stakeholder to some extent. If enough stakeholders are unhappy for a long period of time, management will most likely terminate the project. It's very important for the PM to balance the needs and expectations of all stakeholders to execute a truly successful project.[10]

After all of the hopes, effort, expense, pressure to perform, missed deadlines, and disappointment, what happens when a project fails? How does a failed project affect stakeholders?

The Customer's Point of View

The customer finally realizes that the project team cannot or will not provide quality products and does not use any products that were delivered. The customer's needs remain unmet, and the customer must continue to make do with existing capabilities.

The Effect on Team Members

Members of the failed project team are likely to have worked a lot of extra hours. They feel exhausted, stressed, and empty, having worked for months only to fail in their mission. Colleagues from other parts of their organization may lose respect for them and not want to be associated with them. Team members may worry that they've ruined their reputations within the organization and might start looking for employment elsewhere. When key members of the project team depart, others are likely to become even more discouraged.

The Impact on Business

The customer is likely to have less cash flow and lower productivity and effectiveness in areas affected by the anticipated project. The project developer likely is struggling with increased expenses and losses after adding people to the project in an effort to turn it around.

Blame

Various groups of stakeholders will attempt to determine who is responsible for the failure. There are probably several reasons why the project failed, but no one will want to take responsibility for any of them.

Unwanted Publicity

Both the customer and the developer may receive unwanted, unfavorable publicity that is likely to damage their reputations and negatively affect their future business activities.

In Brief

Projects can fail for a number of reasons, including poorly defined requirements, scope creep, stakeholders' contradictory or unrealistic expectations, lack of demand for the product being made, lack of user involvement in the project, poor or nonexistent change management, poor quality control, and failure to catch problems until it is too late. The underlying problem in all of these situations is the lack of an effective plan or failure to continually update the plan as the project is executed. Typical metrics are not effective because these measures are lagging indicators that do not draw attention to problems until it is too late to solve them easily.

Stakeholder groups have different perspectives, and different stakeholders use differing criteria to evaluate the success of a project. The PM must understand the needs of these groups and must tailor communications to each group to address its expectations. The failure to maintain communications or manage expectations can result in a failed project. When a project fails, there is a huge mess left to clean up. Customers' needs will go unmet, project team members' reputations may be damaged, and the project developer may struggle financially and be subject to negative publicity.

In later chapters, you'll learn that effective planning involves more than developing a schedule and budget and monitoring them using typical metrics. Effective planning also requires identifying the products to be provided and estimating the resources needed to develop them.

Suggested Reading and Resources

Gilb, Tom, and Dorothy Graham. *Software Inspection.* **Reading, MA: Addison-Wesley, 1993.** Importantly for PMs, this book addresses inspections of *any* work product, not just software. The authors' approach is very rigorous, requiring more training and costing more than normal peer reviews. However, it results in earlier correction of defects, which saves money later in the development cycle. This book is invaluable for an organization that is committed to using inspections of work products—a proven method with good payback.[11]

Kharbanda, Om Prakash, and Jeffrey K. Pinto. *What Made Gertie Gallop: Learning From Project Failures.* **New York: Van Nostrand Reinhold Company, 1996.** The title of this book refers to the Tacoma Narrows Bridge, which was known as "Galloping Gertie" because it had a disconcerting tendency to move and shake while it was erected. The bridge ultimately collapsed in the fall of 1940. In this book, Kharbanda and Pinto provide several real-world examples of project failures, highlight reasons why projects fail, describe constraints managers face, identify key principles for project success, and address the reasons why PMs fail to plan properly. Readers can use the book to help identify project risks and develop risk-mitigation strategies as part of the project planning process.

Six Sigma Qualtec. *QI Story: Tools and Techniques, A Guidebook to Problem Solving,* **3rd ed. Tempe, AZ: Six Sigma Qualtec, 1999.** This tiny reference book provides a concise and helpful description of the concepts of total quality management and an overview of the seven-step quality improvement (QI) story. It also includes summaries of QI tools and techniques such as brainstorming, multi-voting, the Pareto chart, the Ishikawa (fishbone) diagram, countermeasures (solutions), cost-benefit analysis, barriers-and-aids analysis, graphs, histograms, process flow charts, and control charts. Visit www.ssqi.com to order a copy.

Wiegers, Karl E. *Peer Reviews in Software: A Practical Guide.* **Boston: Addison-Wesley, 2002.** Wiegers provides a practical and experience-based approach for peer reviews. It includes a chapter on inspections that provides sufficient guidance to begin using this valuable technique. The "Goodies" section of the author's website, www.processimpact.com, offers free document templates, spreadsheets, and more.

Wiegers, Karl E. *Practical Project Initiation.* **Redmond, WA: Microsoft Press, 2007.** This book is recommended reading for any project manager who is about to start a new project. Wiegers has many years of experience and valuable insights and suggestions. In this book, he provides simple but valuable tools that will help readers make their project start-up process more effective and efficient. A feature of the book is the use of icons to denote true stories from real projects and also common project initiation traps to avoid.

Young, Ralph R. *Effective Requirements Practices.* **Boston: Addison-Wesley, 2001.** This book recommends and describes a set of ten effective requirements practices that should be used for any project, system, or software development effort. It also addresses managerial and technical issues that determine the success or failure of a project. The suggested approach helps the PM redirect resources to satisfy customers' and users' real needs. Together, the recommended practices help keep projects on the right track. The book emphasizes the PM's role; working with people on projects; selecting methods, techniques, and tools; and project communication.

Young, Ralph R. *Project Requirements: A Guide to Best Practices.* **Vienna, VA: Management Concepts, 2006.** Written for the program or project manager, this book makes a case for investing in the requirements process and explains how to make the needed investment. Every project should incorporate the industry-proven set of best practices recommended in this book. This book also provides extensive references and resources for additional help, as well as concise appendixes with invaluable guidance on requirements traceability, meeting minimum requirements, and writing a project vision and scope document.

Young, Ralph R. *The Requirements Engineering Handbook.* **Boston: Artech House, 2004.** This book provides guidance for requirements analysts, requirements managers, and others who are assigned responsibilities related to project requirements. Because requirements are the basis for all other work performed on a project, project teams are more much more likely to succeed if they perform requirements-related tasks and work effectively. It is both unfortunate and amazing that industry practices have not improved in spite of the compelling evidence that poor requirements work is a root cause of project failures.

Notes

1. Steve McConnell, *Software Estimation: Demystifying the Black Art* (Redmond, WA: Microsoft Press, 2006).
2. Ibid., 27.
3. Capers Jones, "Software Project Management Practices: Failure Versus Success." *CrossTalk: The Journal of Defense Software Engineering* 17 (October 2004): 5–9.
4. A project champion is an advocate of the project who is very familiar with customer requirements and who provides an active and vocal role

in the development effort. The project champion defends the project when necessary, for example, from the project sponsor (the person or organization prioritizing funding for the project) and from critics of the project.

5. See Ralph R. Young, *The Requirements Engineering Handbook* (Boston: Artech House, 2004): 65–67, for a discussion of how to identify project stakeholders. For a more extensive treatment, go to www.scenarioplus .org.uk/download_stakeholders.html; the "Onion" Model of Stakeholders may be of use.

6. See Ralph R. Young, *Project Requirements: A Guide to Best Practices* (Vienna, VA: Management Concepts, 2006): Appendix C, for a project vision and scope document template.

7. See Ralph R. Young, *Effective Requirements Practices* (Boston: Addison-Wesley, 2001): 58–91, for a detailed discussion of how to evolve stated requirements into real requirements.

8. Ibid.

9. Honesty is one of the most powerful tools a PM can have. See Steven Gaffney, *Just Be Honest: Authentic Communication Strategies That Get Results and Last a Lifetime* (Arlington, VA: JMG Publishing, 2002). This book describes why honesty is the easiest and most effective way to communicate. Honesty will provide immediate and dramatic results with anyone, regardless of their background, needs, personality, or personal agenda. See also www.honestcommunication.com for more valuable resources to help improve communications and establish genuine relationships, trust, and support with colleagues.

10. See Karl E. Wiegers, "See You In Court," *Software Development Magazine* 11.1 (January 2003), for a discussion of several practices that might help you balance and maintain the needs and expectations of all stakeholders.

11. Rob Sabourin (rsabourin@amibug.com) offers an economical inspections training and implementation approach.

2 Is Your Project Out of Control?

A frustrated PM wondered out loud how his project had gotten out of control. A seasoned colleague replied, "One day at a time." Even if we try to do our best each day at work, sometimes things just don't come together, and projects go in the wrong direction. How do you know if your project is out of control? Some common indicators include:

- Missed milestones or deliverables

- Lack of product quality

- Different opinions of the project's purpose

- Failure to estimate costs and schedule in advance

- Dependence on heroes

- Customer disapproval

- Employee frustration

- Other subtle signs of trouble.

Most of these indicators are *lagging*. In other words, problems are discovered only after they happen, and the project still must spend money and time fixing the problems. A *leading indicator* uncovers a potential problem before it happens. The project is able to save resources by correcting the issue before it turns into a problem. By learning about and using indicators, especially leading indicators, your project team may recognize problems early enough to stay within budget and schedule.

▬▬ Missed Milestones or Deliverables

All projects should have a documented plan that includes a schedule for selected milestones (such as the requirements review, completion of the design, and completion of engineering activities) and also for various deliverables (such as the requirements document, the design document, and finished engineering products). An early indicator that the project may be slipping is difficulty in meeting scheduled milestones and delivering high-quality work products.

It's all too easy to lose a lot of time in the early phases of a project. This is often because many activities need to be addressed, including obtaining needed resources (such as facilities and space, people, and equipment); establishing coordination and communication with the customer; arranging meetings; clarifying customer needs and requirements; developing subcontractor agreements; writing various plans and documents (including finalizing the contract); obtaining needed training; and orienting staff to the project environment and customer. The list seems endless, and some time-consuming detail seems to pop up every day!

Early in a project, there isn't much pressure to make substantial progress. Once the PM and the project management team realize that time is passing quickly, they become concerned. A better approach would be to start the project on day one with a sense of serious purpose and an expectation of effectiveness and productivity each day. The PM must invest in development of a detailed project plan, and managers must pay attention to project activities. Create and maintain an action item list to help hold project team members accountable for their duties.

Sometimes, missed milestones and deliverables are a natural result of an unreasonable top-down schedule being imposed on the project team, perhaps to meet an arbitrary goal, such as a time-to-market goal. This schedule may have been thrown together during the initial stages of the project by people not on the team. It's important for the members of the project team to develop their own schedule; this will encourage their commitment to meeting the milestones.

Lack of Product Quality

Often there is pressure to complete a deliverable according to schedule. Some pressure is positive—it encourages us to be productive and reach our goals. But if pressure makes completing a deliverable with high quality standards impossible, it is negative and unreasonable. (By "high quality standards," we mean that the deliverable is free of defects and fully meets the requirements.)

Different Opinions of the Project's Purpose

Fostering and maintaining good communications on projects is difficult, and it is further complicated by the fact that each person involved brings different experiences, expertise, and perspective. People supporting the project will naturally have different opinions of the target—the purpose and objectives of the project. (Recall the discussion from Chapter 1 and Figure 1-2.) Take time and effort at the beginning of the project to ensure that the real requirements[1] have been evolved and to brief all project staff on the goals and objectives of the project. This will help ensure a common understanding of the target.

Failure to Estimate Costs and Schedule in Advance

It's challenging to estimate costs and schedule in advance, and it's impossible without taking the time and effort to develop a detailed project plan that identifies all of the products that need to be created, both external products (deliverables) and internal products. Although techniques such as earned-value management have been developed to help track cost and schedule, these techniques have not been very effective.[2]

Dependence on Heroes

Many projects are dependent on one or a few project staff members who are particularly effective and committed to the project's success.

This is a dangerous practice—what will happen if for some reason these heroes are no longer available? A better approach is to staff the project with qualified people, provide them needed training, familiarize them with the project's goals and objectives, and establish the expectation that everyone do his or her fair share of the work.

Customer Disapproval

A key indicator that your project may be spiraling out of control is customer concern or disapproval. It's essential to stay close to your customers. You must be aware of their concerns and show that you care by making immediate and proactive efforts to address any problems. Be sure to tell customers what you've done to alleviate their concerns. Too often, customers' worries become deeply rooted before they share them with the PM.

Employee Frustration

Employees become frustrated for many reasons:

- Lack of appreciation or recognition
- Lack of clearly articulated project goals and objectives
- Unfulfilling assignments that make the employee feel as if he or she is wasting time and effort
- Being expected to work extra hours on a regular basis, on weekends, or during holidays
- Being asked—or told—to cancel a scheduled vacation or family event
- An unsupportive project environment that is not team-oriented
- Lack of regular communication and comprehensive information.

An effective PM provides strong leadership, communicates clearly and regularly, and sets a good example for the project team. He or she has realistic expectations and ensures that project milestones are met.

Other Subtle Signs of Trouble

Less obvious indicators that problems are developing may include:

- *Requests from the customer to make additions or changes to requirements. Requirements creep,* sometimes called *requirements churn,* frequently causes loss of control on projects. The project should track *requirements volatility* (the number of changes to requirements plus new requirements, divided by the total number of requirements) on a monthly basis and ensure that it does not exceed 2 percent each month.[3]

- *Staff attrition.* When staff members leave a project, it's important to understand why. The PM should work to ensure that every staff member is satisfied with the work he or she is doing; team members should leave work most days with a feeling of accomplishment. PMs should also provide or inform staff members about opportunities for professional development and training.

- *Tension during meetings.* The project staff should be working as an empowered team. This means that each person has the authority to make decisions within his or her level of responsibility and that team members actively support each other. If exchanges during project meetings are acerbic, the PM might consider taking steps to improve teamwork—for example, creating a set of Rules of Conduct (see Figure 2-1 for a sample set).

- *Surprises.* There should be few surprises, such as frequent changes in project direction or funding, that disrupt the project.

- *Lack of trust.* A strong commitment to the project's success, mutual respect, and trust are indicators of a healthy project and project team. A lack of trust may suggest instability or uncertainty.

FIGURE 2-1: Sample Rules of Conduct

- Prepare for the meeting
- Arrive on time
- Limit individual contributions to focused, constructive inputs
- Share responsibility for successful outcomes
- Criticize ideas and concepts, not people
- Respect each person
- Support one another
- Be open to new ideas and change
- Avoid whining—e.g., "We tried that already!"
- Review action items and ensure a common understanding of meeting results
- Complete assigned action items on time
- Communicate early and often; confirm understanding
- Manage by facts, using data, rather than by intuition
- Perform Plan-Do-Check-Act (PDCA) at the end of each meeting. Give each participant an opportunity to make suggestions about how the team can do better.

- *Lack of honest feedback.* This can undermine relationships and reduce the project staff's effectiveness.

- *Lack of management support.* This might be indicated by management's requesting completion in advance of the original deadline. Both management and developer should agree on a scheduled deadline, and both should commit to meeting that deadline. If the customer pressures management to change the deadline, management must take a stand and support the developer. The developer must make every effort to meet the deadline as well.

- *Consistently operating in "crisis mode,"* which indicates lack of planning.

- *Finger-pointing.* Poor communication and individuals' resistance to being held accountable can cause various project groups to blame others for their own problems.

- *Defects in delivered work products.* Peer reviews, quality assurance reviews, and defect-prevention processes should eliminate most defects before the customer finds them.

- *Frequent rework.* The average amount of rework on projects is 50 percent! The project should strive to minimize rework, keeping it to perhaps 10 percent, by striving for and establishing a habit of continuous improvement of project processes.

- *Declaring incomplete work products "done."* We cannot adhere to the schedule at the expense of product quality.

- *Poor assumptions.* Projects are too often planned on the basis of assumptions that were not articulated or that turn out to be invalid.

- *Project risks aren't mitigated.* Every project should maintain a risk register that describes risks, identifies the risk owner (responsible party), assigns a value to each risk based on the probability that it will occur and the severity of its possible impact, and quantifies the resulting risk exposure. The project's risk review board should determine how to mitigate risks that have a high risk exposure value. If the mitigation actions cannot be executed, difficulty may lie ahead—thus, the need for contingency plans.

- *Ineffective meetings.* Each project staff member's time is valuable. Ineffective project meetings waste time and send the wrong message to staff members. The meeting organizer should distribute an agenda for each meeting beforehand. Meetings should start and end on time. Assign someone to monitor discussion and speak up when too much time is spent on one topic or the discussion is getting off-topic. Allow a few minutes at the end of each meeting for each participant to offer an observation or suggestion for improvement.

- *Delayed decisions.* To keep a project moving as scheduled, timely decisions are necessary. Postponing important decisions can hurt the project.

- *Counterproductive responses to bad news.* Managers should expect to be informed when problems arise and should be prepared to suggest alternative approaches when needed. When a problem has been identified and shared with him or her, the manager must respond positively. After all, the sooner a problem is identified and communicated, the earlier it can be addressed. "Shooting the messenger"—becoming angry with the person who identifies or communicates a problem—is damaging. Managers who take this approach eventually won't be informed of problems at all.

Regaining Control

There are usually multiple indicators that a project is out of control. It's easy to pretend that these indicators are not critical and simply trust that things will work out, but to regain control of the project, managers may need to take action or ask for help from others. If your project is out of control, it is best to stop and regroup. Working faster and harder may continue or even worsen the uncontrolled spiral. First, confirm that those who are sponsoring (paying for) the project still want the project to proceed. If so, enlist help from external project management and process improvement experts to help your project team formulate a realistic plan.

In Brief

Risk factors that threaten projects' stability and viability include missed milestones or deliverables, poor product quality, stakeholders having different opinions of the project's purpose, failure to estimate costs and schedule in advance, dependence on heroes, customer disapproval, employee frustration, and subtler signs of trouble, such as requirements creep, staff attrition, poor communication, and surprises. If your project is beset by several of these problems, stop the project and regroup. The next three chapters outline your next steps. They explain how to analyze a troubled project by determining its objectives and goals and whether it can move forward; the purpose and elements of a project plan; and how to build a plan that will effectively guide your work over the lifetime of your project.

Suggested Reading and Resources

Kerth, Norman L. *Project Retrospectives: A Handbook for Team Reviews.* New York: Dorset House Publishing, 2001. One way to develop a greater understanding of how and why projects lose control is to write a project retrospective (also known as a post mortem, after action review, lessons learned report, case study, and other terms) after the project is finished. A project retrospective is an organized review of a project to reflect on what went well and what went badly, learn from these experiences, and plan for changes during the next project. The key is to ensure that the review results in positive and effective changes to future projects. See www.retrospectives. com for more information.

Solomon, Paul J., and Ralph R. Young. *Performance-Based Earned Value.* **Hoboken, NJ: John Wiley & Sons, 2007.** Traditional earned value and earned-value management techniques have often not served projects well. This book proposes a change to industry practice—making earned value performance-based. It details how to effectively integrate technical, schedule, and cost objectives; provides guidelines, methods, examples, and templates; and explains how to incorporate a performance-based approach on a project. The book describes technical performance measures and explains how they are selected, monitored, and reported. It explains how to integrate risk management procedures and discusses how to implement the performance-based approach relative to the federal acquisition regulations.

Notes

1. See Ralph R. Young, *Effective Requirements Practices* (Boston: Addison-Wesley, 2001): 58–91, for a detailed discussion of how to evolve stated requirements into real requirements.
2. See Paul J. Solomon and Ralph R. Young, *Performance-Based Earned Value* (Hoboken, NJ: John Wiley & Sons, 2007), for a better earned-value approach that is based on the successful completion of work products rather than on the amount of effort that has been performed.
3. Capers Jones notes that the ability to measure requirements creep "explains why function point metrics are now starting to become the basis of software contracts and outsource agreements." ("Preventing Software Failure: Problems Noted in Breach of Contract Litigation," October 2008, p. 4.)

II

Project Planning
How to Recover a Failing Project

3 Analyzing Your Project

Proper planning in the early stages of a project is essential to its success. Planning that does not address the goals and objectives of the project in sufficient detail is a root cause of failing projects.

If your project is foundering, and you didn't devise an adequate plan at the beginning, now is the time to do so. Plans should be based on the business objectives that must be met and the functional goals of the completed project. *Functional goals* are the specific products and services that meet the needs and expectations of users. Once you've reviewed the objectives and the functional goals of the project, you can decide whether to move forward with the project. After developing the project plan, pay close attention to process and procedure development. This will further boost your chances of success.

Assessing Why Your Project Is Failing

In Chapter 1, we discussed the reasons projects fail. Consider these thoughtfully, and evaluate why your project is having problems. It's likely that there is more than one reason. Think about the relative importance of each reason. This process will help you realize what must change if the project is to succeed.

Defining the Business Objectives the Project Should Meet

Projects are undertaken to address and meet business objectives. *Business objectives* address and support the purpose of performing work and the needs of those for whom the work is done. Analyzing and evaluating the business objectives is essential. Some are more important than others, so it makes good business sense to prioritize them and develop a project approach that addresses the most significant objectives first.

Project work should be performed with attention to *return on investment (ROI),* which is the value gained from using the capital provided by a business owner (or the shareholders of a corporation). Business owners or shareholders demand a favorable ROI in order for them to be willing to make capital available.

Defining the Functional Goals the Project Should Satisfy

Your project will likely suffer if the functional goals that it is supposed to satisfy have not been defined in sufficient detail. To design, develop, and implement a project, functional goals must be defined as specifically and precisely as possible. This makes it possible for developers to fully understand and address what they need to do.

Functional goals may be refined into one or more verifiable requirements. A *requirement* is a necessary attribute in a system. Each requirement for a system identifies a capability, characteristic, or quality factor that offers value and utility to a user. To evolve a complete set of requirements, you must identify all of your project's stakeholders to ensure that no one and nothing is left out. Then prioritize the requirements; it's not possible to do everything the stakeholders want. A systematic requirements process must be used in order to define the functional goals effectively.[1]

Deciding Whether To Move Forward

Once you have determined that your project is failing, you can either cancel the project or restart it.[2] Those who are funding the project may want to reevaluate whether the need for the system being developed is compelling enough to continue the project. To facilitate this decision, a comprehensive analysis of the vision and scope of the project should be done (or refined, if one already exists).[3]

What if the scope of the failing project is too broad or too vague? At this point, the scope of the project can be refocused on the most critical business objectives and the prioritized functional goals. Determine why the project is struggling, and decide how you are going to correct the underlying problems.

Encouraging Management's Positive Involvement

In our experience, problems caused by management issues are more common than purely technical problems. The customer's senior managers must be strong, vocal project sponsors and must stay involved in the project as it evolves. Senior managers can facilitate progress by participating in regular reviews, for example. Managers should be available to provide advice and facilitate decisions and should look for opportunities to assist the project. Consider forming a project steering committee composed of representatives of key stakeholders. Committee meetings will help all parties stay apprised of project activities and progress.

If you are a senior manager or an advisor, be an active listener and keep an open mind. Ensure that your own expectations do not influence what others are willing to tell you. If a developer knows that you want to hear only good news, he or she may not give you a truthful, accurate rundown of the project's status and progress. Make clear that you are interested in an honest assessment of the situation and particularly in how you or others might be able to help.[4]

Performing Process and Procedure Development

Most project teams fail to document the processes and procedures used to perform work and create products, but such documentation yields clear benefits.

- The project team learns from the perspective and experience of those who are actually performing each process or procedure.

- Documentation enables continuous improvement of the process or procedure.

- Documentation ensures that everyone involved in performing a process or procedure has the same understanding of it.

- Documentation encourages buy-in to processes and procedures because team members have a role in their development.

Planning

When creating a project plan, the project team identifies processes and procedures required to implement the plan. It's essential that the team members commit to using the documented processes and procedures to perform the work. Too often, project team members rely on their own understanding of a process or procedure, which may not be an understanding shared by others on the team. This approach often leads to chaos.

Requirements Development and Management

Perhaps the two most prevalent problems when performing requirements development and management are:

- Failure to identify the real requirements before performing other technical work

- Failure to control changes to requirements and new requirements that are identified as the project proceeds.

Take time to document the project's requirements process to help ward off these root causes of requirements-related problems and project failure. The project team can both reduce rework and greatly improve its probability of success by asking key stakeholders to help create a flow chart that describes the requirements process, creating a joint team to take responsibility for the requirements, and using best practices such as writing a vision and scope document and prioritizing requirements.

Peer Reviews

Peer reviews are among the most powerful project processes. They help identify defects (for example, omitted requirements in a requirements document) earlier, which saves time and effort, reduces costs, helps the team stay on schedule, and boosts quality. Peer reviews build quality into the way work is performed and the project's products and deliverables.

A peer review is a defined process by which the developer's peers analyze a product with the specific goal of identifying problems. The peers may be members of the project team or other members of the developer's company who have the expertise necessary to review the product.

The process is simple. The reviewers inspect the product using a predefined checklist of specific aspects to review. If a problem is found, the reviewer records the problem in a provided template. When the inspection is complete, each reviewer makes a recommendation regarding the product, choosing from options that often include the following:

- Accept the product as-is—no additional changes are needed.

- Accept the product conditionally—the product will be sufficient after all the problems are corrected.

- Re-review—the reviewers want to re-review the product after changes are made.

- Rebuild—the reviewers believe that the product should be disposed of and completely rebuilt from scratch.

After the review, the reviewers and the developer meet to ensure the developer understands any problems well enough to fix them. See Chapter 13 for more information about peer reviews.

Defect Prevention

Defect prevention (DP), which addresses and attempts to fix a project's trouble spots, is another simple and very powerful process that should be used on all projects.

1. The relevant project team members brainstorm possible root causes of the problems. They discuss how each root cause is affecting the project and then vote to reach consensus on the relative importance of each root cause.

2. The group then prioritizes the root causes and brainstorms measures to mitigate the effects of the three to five most significant root causes.

3. The team members discuss the potential impact of each countermeasure and select the most effective countermeasures by vote.

4. The group decides how to implement the countermeasures and how to measure and track their effects.

5. After a reasonable period of time, the group evaluates the impact of the selected countermeasures and decides whether to continue using them or try others that might be more effective.

A small group of project members can accomplish this work quickly, and it can have an enormous positive effect on the project's outcome.

Quantitative Management

Most managers are not familiar with quantitative management (QM). QM is a management technique that involves using statistical process control (SPC) to assess the capability of processes. It is powerful and easier to apply than one might think. See Chapter 13 for additional discussion of QM.[5]

Change Management

Mechanisms must be put in place to control change on projects. Mechanisms to manage change include baselines, versions and releases of products and deliverables, and updated or new subsystems. Remember that a project can't deliver everything to everyone.

Requirements workshops can help stakeholders understand other stakeholders' needs and can help teams prioritize requirements. A requirements workshop is a structured meeting in which a carefully selected group of stakeholders and content experts work together to define, create, refine, and reach closure on deliverables that represent user requirements.[6] Requirements workshops are invaluable in enabling different stakeholders to understand the needs of others.

Changing the Culture of a Project

A project's culture may impede project success. For example, if the members of the project team are stuck in their ways and are not interested in process improvement, they may resist changes to the development process that could improve deliverables. Members of the project team need leadership and direction from the PM to know how to use processes, communicate openly, and contribute their best efforts.

Three resources that provide extensive help in this area are Rita Hadden's *Leading Culture Change in Your Software Organization,* Karl Wiegers' *Creating a Software Engineering Culture,* and Neal Whitten's *No-Nonsense Advice for Successful Projects.* (For more information on these resources, please see the suggested reading section of this chapter.)

In his more recent book, *Neal Whitten's Let's Talk! More No-Nonsense Advice for Project Success,* Whitten advises PMs to deliver a culture training class to all project members to familiarize the team with key hard skills, soft skills, and processes that are essential to project success.[7] For example, Whitten notes that hard skills are mostly process- and procedure-oriented, such as the mechanics of the development life cycle, tracking, risk assessments, and project reviews. Soft skills are more behavior-oriented and include leading, directing, nurturing, and mitigating.[8] Critical processes include project planning, project tracking, the escalation process, and the post-project review.[9]

In Brief

Planning should be based on the business objectives that must be met and the functional goals of the completed project. If project teams want to succeed, they must focus on proper planning, then on process and procedure development. PMs often believe that such effort is unnecessary, but in our experience, the failure to develop (or adapt from others' experience and existing documents) processes, procedures, and checklists is a root cause of project problems.

Suggested Reading and Resources

Cagle, Ronald B. *Blueprint for Project Recovery: The Complete Process for Getting Derailed Projects Back on Track.* New York: AMACOM, 2003. Addresses topics of interest to PMs, including discussion of vendor evaluation and selection; data-organization techniques; a contract/subcontract outline; a sample standards traceability matrix (to complement the requirements traceability matrix); and a negotiation checklist that helps the PM outline needs and wants before beginning negotiations.

Electronic Industries Alliance (EIA). *ANSI/EIA 632, Processes for Engineering a System.* Arlington, VA: EIA, 1998. This valuable standard provides a comprehensive, structured, disciplined approach for all life cycle phases of a project. The systems engineering process is applied iteratively. The publication discusses industry initiatives to identify and integrate requirements and to implement multidisciplinary teamwork, including working with potential suppliers. The standard also encourages innovation in products and practices and urges project teams to establish clear measurements and to focus on process control.

Hadden, Rita Chao. *Leading Culture Change in Your Software Organization: Delivering Results Early.* Vienna, VA: Management Concepts, 2003.

This book focuses on the leadership required to achieve lasting process improvement and change the culture of a project. It is very useful for a PM who's faced with the need to improve the way his or her organization does business. The book offers examples, insights, success stories, and lessons learned from other projects. (Note that "lessons learned" are those we actually *apply* in our own work environment! Lessons are too often observed without application later.)

McConnell, Steve. "The Power of Process." *Computer* **31 (May 1998): 100–102.** Many PMs resist investing in the development or tailoring of processes and in process improvement. This article by an industry expert offers a compelling argument for paying attention to processes. Projects get into trouble when they don't have effective (documented and repeatable) processes for activities such as requirements development and management, project planning, project tracking, controlling changes, peer reviews, defect tracking, quality assurance, configuration management, and product implementation. Effective processes eliminate many project problems and make it easier to perform the work. McConnell reports that the average cost of process improvement is about 2 percent of total development costs, or about $1,500 per developer per year. He believes that an environment of continuous improvement can be fostered without limiting developers' creativity and that a process-focused approach and the resulting productivity increase staff morale. The article is available at www.stevemcconnell. com/articles/art09.htm.

McDonald, Marc, Robert Musson, and Ross Smith. *The Practical Guide to Defect Prevention.* **Redmond, WA: Microsoft Press, 2008.** If you are serious about preventing software defects before they occur, this guide provides extensive background, experience, guidance, techniques—such as how to perform root-cause analysis—and best practices. The authors address integrating prevention techniques into Agile and CMMI frameworks.

Purba, Sanjiv, and Joseph J. Zucchero. *Project Rescue: Avoiding a Project Management Disaster.* **New York: Osborne McGraw-Hill, 2004.** This book complements our own approach. The authors provide early detection questions and an assessment questionnaire that will help you conduct a comprehensive evaluation of your project's situation. The authors provide examples of important project processes, including risk management, establishing a management control office, conflict management, and issue management. They emphasize the value of a project charter and formal written procedures for critical areas, including project planning and tracking, requirements, quality assurance, communications, change management, scope management, estimation of project work and work products, and acceptance management.

Weller, Ed. "Practical Applications of Statistical Process Control," *Proceedings of the 10th International Conference on Software Quality,* **July 2000.** This excellent article explains how to use SPC to improve project success. Applying quantitative methods and SPC to development projects can provide a positive cost-benefit return. Quantitative analysis of inspection and test data is used to analyze product quality during testing and to predict post-ship product quality for a major release. The article describes the processes, decisions, and results of the analysis. The author advises readers to ask two questions about any metric or analysis technique: 1) Is it useful—does it provide information that helps make decisions? 2) Is it useable—can it help users reasonably collect the data and conduct an analysis?

Whitten, Neal. *Neal Whitten's No-Nonsense Advice for Successful Projects.* **Vienna, VA: Management Concepts, 2005.** Whitten has 30 years of experience in managing projects and teaching and consulting about project management. In this book, he shares his experiences and lessons learned as a PM, including discussions of project planning, project execution and control, project initiation, roles and responsibilities, and leadership.

Whitten, Neal. *Neal Whitten's Let's Talk! More No-Nonsense Advice for Project Success.* **Vienna, VA: Management Concepts, 2007.** This book builds on the lessons of Whitten's 2005 book. Whitten uses a question-and-answer format to present his ideas about "the people side" of a project, including interpersonal communications, resolving conflict, meetings, celebrations, mentoring, telecommuting, recognition, personal development, and promoting change.

Wiegers, Karl E. *Creating a Software Engineering Culture.* New York: Dorset House, 1996. This book provides a comprehensive approach to improving the quality and effectiveness of the software development process. Wiegers promotes the tactical changes required to support process improvement and high-quality software development. He identifies "culture builders" and "culture killers." A section entitled "What to Do on Monday" describes high-impact actions that managers can implement immediately.

Notes

1. See Ralph R. Young, *Effective Requirements Practices* (Boston: Addison-Wesley, 2001): 9–14 and 110–125, for a description of an effective requirements process.
2. See Robert Powell and Dennis Buede, *The Project Manager's Guide to Making Successful Decisions,* for an excellent discussion about making the decision to either cancel or restart a failing project. Chapter 5 provides a decision structure to help you.
3. See Ralph R. Young, *Project Requirements: A Guide to Best Practices* (Vienna, VA: Management Concepts, 2006): Appendix C, for a project vision and scope document template.
4. According to the new Capability Maturity Model® Integration for Services (CMMI-SVC), research has shown that the most powerful initial step to process improvement is to build organizational support through strong senior management sponsorship. See www.sei.cmu.edu/cmmi/models/CMMI-Services-status.html for details about the new model. See also Sarah Sheard's "What Is Senior Management Commitment?," which provides thoughtful advice, suggestions, and recommendations on how to facilitate senior management sponsorship.
5. Managers should make an effort to familiarize themselves with QM. See for example Ed Weller, "Practical Applications of Statistical Process Control," *IEEE Software* v.17, no.3 (May/June 2000), and Donald Wheeler and David Chambers, *Understanding Statistical Process Control,* 2nd ed. (Knoxville, TN: SPC Press, 1992).
6. Ellen Gottesdiener, *Requirements by Collaboration* (Addison-Wesley, 2002): 296. See also www.ebgconsulting.com for extensive information about organizing and conducting a requirements workshop.
7. Neal Whitten, *Neal Whitten's Let's Talk! More No-Nonsense Advice for Project Success* (Vienna, VA: Management Concepts, 2007). See especially Chapter 27.
8. Ibid., 263–264.
9. Ibid., 264.

4 Why Create a Plan?

When we need to drive somewhere we've never been before, most of us go to an Internet mapping site and print directions. We do this to avoid getting lost, wasting our time, and using fuel unnecessarily. Creating a project plan is analogous to printing directions. The project plan is your roadmap to the finish line.

Now, let's say that you're leading a caravan of cars to take your child's ball team to a field in another city. You might provide a copy of the directions for each driver so that everyone in the caravan knows where the team is headed. This is a risk mitigation strategy in case one of the cars is separated from the caravan. The separated driver can still reach the ball field by following his or her own copy of the directions.

Directions also provide milestones. Milestones let you know you're headed in the right direction. Knowing which streets to turn on and the distance to travel on each street gives a driver confidence that he or she is headed in the right direction. As a PM, you should be able to instill in the project's stakeholders confidence that the team is headed in the right direction. By developing and using a plan to guide the project, you can quickly tell if you are off track and can consider taking corrective action. As Figure 4-1 shows, the longer it takes you to realize you're off track, the more costly it is to get back on.

Albert Einstein defined insanity as "doing the same thing over and over again and expecting different results." If your project is in trouble,

FIGURE 4-1: Why Use a Plan?

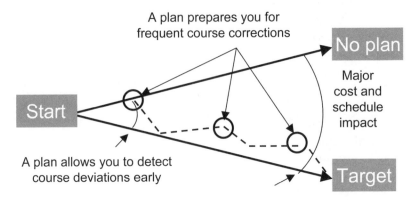

A plan prepares you for
frequent course corrections

No plan

Major
cost and
schedule
impact

Start

A plan allows you to detect
course deviations early

Target

No plan often means you detect
course deviations way too late

you need to set a new course. Showing your project team and the project's stakeholders a new plan is the best way to communicate a change in direction. The plan shows the stakeholders where the project is headed and how you're going to get there. It will help ensure that all stakeholders have a common understanding of the project's goals.

Setting a new course isn't enough. As the PM, it's your job to demonstrate to the stakeholders that the project is following the plan. Tell them what the project milestones are, and as you meet them, let the stakeholders know. This will strengthen their confidence in your project team.

Have you ever driven someplace new and thought you were headed in the right direction only to find out that you were not? A well-built plan will reduce uncertainty about whether the project is headed in the right direction. Plans provide quantifiable size, effort, and time metrics to measure performance, and they allow you to manage based on facts rather than feelings.

To build a plan, you must identify all the products to be produced, estimate the physical size of each product, estimate the time required to create them, assign responsibility for building them, and determine when they're going to be complete. These initial estimates create the baselines by which the project's performance can be measured and tracked.

Experienced PMs know that projects rarely proceed as initially planned; they often change dramatically. Resources are added and removed, requirements change, miscommunications occur, and stakeholders forget key information. A plan helps you manage the project as the circumstances surrounding the project change.

Let's say you're following written directions on a road trip. Everything is going according to plan—until you hit a roadblock. Now you must take an alternate route. Similarly, throughout the course of a project, you'll encounter roadblocks. When you do, you'll need to replan so that the plan continues to guide the work. By updating the plan as changes occur, you can use it to help control the effects of each change—rather than allowing change to control you.

In this chapter, we talk about the importance of building a plan and explain how to use the plan to create a single vision for all stakeholders. We explain how to build a plan and show you how fact-based management helps keep stakeholders informed and confident. Finally, we discuss the importance of maintaining the plan throughout the life of the project in order to control the inevitable project changes.

Creating a Single Vision

We developed the concept for this book after our manager received a call from another manager in our company who had just inherited a troubled $250 million firm-fixed-price project. This project's team consisted of over 80 people, including 15 different team leaders. Our manager asked us to help the project team, which was over budget, had made a poor-quality product, had just fired the previous PM, and had an unhappy customer. During the first week we worked with the project team, we conducted an assessment of the project, just as we discussed in Chapter 3. One of our key findings from the analysis was that each of the 15 team leaders worked only with those on his or her sub-team instead of communicating with everyone on the main project team. These leaders did not really understand how their sub-teams' work fit into the overall project. This created a fragmented team that lacked the vision and focus to successfully complete the project.

We found that the 80-person team was technically talented, worked hard, and worked many extra hours. We knew that if we could rechannel the team's efforts and get its members to work together toward a single vision, we could take advantage of their talents and turn the project around. After completing our analysis, we asked the team to stop most of its current efforts so that we could develop an integrated project plan that supported the entire project team.

We then gathered the project's external stakeholders and told them what we wanted to do and how we were going to do it. The project team was surprised to learn that the customer thought replanning the project was a great idea. In fact, the customer had already realized that the project was heading in the wrong direction and was struggling to come up with ideas on how to fix the problems.

As we re-planned the project, our goal was to create a single vision of the finish line. To accomplish this, we needed to align all of the stakeholders' goals and expectations. We solicited participation from all of the stakeholders, including our company's staff and the customer's senior management team. We then structured the replanning team with representation from each group.

The Plan Components

As we worked with the project's stakeholders, it became clear that many thought that a Microsoft Project schedule equaled or provided a project plan. This is a common misconception. We realized that we needed to educate the team about what a plan contains, each component's purpose, and how long a good plan would take to develop.

First, we explained to the team that the plan's purpose was to guide *all* of the work. If the plan didn't identify all of the required work, the project team would automatically begin behind schedule—because the work still had to be completed even if it was not accounted for in the plan. This would force the project team to add additional resources or adjust the schedule. We then talked about the interrelationships between the project sub-teams, providing a clear understanding of what each sub-team was doing and how each related to the others. This helped the project team members better appreciate the importance of their jobs and the effect their work had on other groups.

We then discussed the components that make up a plan and some of the key components needed to feed the development of the plan. These include:

- *Product breakdown structure (PBS):* This tool is used to identify all the products the project team needs to create in the course of executing the project. The project plan must account for all the products described in the PBS.

- *Work breakdown structure (WBS):* This tool is used to identify all the work the project team needs to perform to execute the project. The WBS is critical to understanding the types of resources required during the course of the project.

- *The project overview:* This section of the plan describes what the project is and defines the project's objectives. It gives all of the stakeholders a clear understanding of the project's mission.

- *A build process model (BPM):* The build process model describes the high-level processes that the team will use to execute the project. The BPM also defines the interactions between the sub-teams and their respective processes and deliverables.

- *Process definitions:* This section of the plan defines all of the individual processes that the project sub-teams will use. These include requirements management, change management, development, testing, and deployment, to name a few.

- *Project organizational structure:* This section of the plan includes an organization chart that lists the roles and responsibilities of each project team member.

- *Resource-loaded schedule:* A resource-loaded schedule assigns project resources to specific tasks. It accounts for all project work, including due dates, costs, and work assignments. As you can imagine, this part of the plan draws a lot of scrutiny from the project stakeholders, which is why some think that a schedule is the same thing as a plan. We explain in detail how to build a project schedule in Chapter 9.

The Plan Development Process

The process you'll go through to develop the plan and all of its components is called the plan development process (PDP). The PDP is typically led by the PM, with participation from team leads, and can include members of the project team on staff at the time. As new team members are hired, they should be included in the PDP process as well, until the plan is complete.

1. Begin by establishing the project's mission statement, which includes its goals and objectives.

2. Identify all of the products that the project is going to produce and all of the work to be performed. (*Products* are any tangible item that will be produced as a result of doing the project. Products can be almost anything: documents, plans, designs, software programs, buildings, or meeting minutes.) Understanding the products and the type of work to be accomplished on the project will help you identify the skills prospective team members must possess.

3. Develop the project's organizational hierarchy, including roles and responsibilities.

4. Once the hierarchy is established, identify specific individuals who have the skills to fill each role.

5. After defining the products and the work to be done and selecting the team, you will be able to develop the resource-loaded schedule.

The key driver of the plan's development is the identification of the project's products and work. In fact, the identification of products and work is so important to the planning process that we have dedicated entire chapters in this book to each activity. Chapter 7 teaches you how to develop a product breakdown structure (PBS). The PBS is a tool developed by the planning team to identify and capture all of the products, their respective sizes, and quality requirements. Chapter 8 teaches you how to develop a work breakdown structure (WBS). The WBS is a tool developed by the planning team to identify all of the work and estimate its duration. The work listed is linked to the products listed in the PBS. The PBS and WBS must be created early in the PDP so that the planning team can use the knowledge gained by developing these documents to build the best plan.

Fact-based Management

Fact-based management is the key to ensuring the team is headed in the right direction, building stakeholder confidence, and communicating project status and needs. When you create the PBS and WBS, you will decompose the project into small, measurable components of work spanning hours and days, not weeks and months. This level of detail is then built into the project's plan to measure project performance and adherence to the plan.

Let's start by looking at how fact-based management can be used to effectively communicate the project's needs. Have you ever approached management to ask for resources to complete a project? You've probably noticed that they often try to give you less than you think you need. If you haven't identified all of the products to be produced and all of the work to be accomplished, it is difficult to defend your request. If management does not give you the resources necessary to execute the project because you couldn't prove you needed them or weren't aware that you did, your project will be behind schedule from the start.

Now imagine meeting with management to ask for resources after you've developed a PBS and WBS. The PBS and WBS identify the resource needs of the project. The conversation can now be conducted based on facts. You can tell your management team exactly what the project must produce and how much work will be needed to make the products. Now, instead of subjectively trying to defend your resource needs, you can discuss them in terms of the detailed lists of products and work.

Fact-based management can also be used to give project stakeholders early warning when the project gets off course. To illustrate the importance of early identification of a problem, let's say you're driving from one city to another. If you miss an exit you were supposed to take but realize it quickly and take an alternate route as soon as possible, you can be back on track in a few minutes. But if you don't realize that you've missed the exit until an hour has passed, it will take a much longer to correct your mistake. Fact-based management can be used throughout a project to identify the need for small corrections, when they are much easier and quicker to make.

Here's an example of how we used fact-based management to identify and correct a problem with one of our projects. We were leading a software development project to produce 32 different detailed design folders; each design folder had a required test folder. Each test folder was expected to take an average of 24 hours to produce, so we estimated that it would take 768 hours to produce all 32 folders. By tracking the production of each test folder, we realized after developing just a few folders that it was really taking an average of 40 hours to develop each one, and to complicate matters, the defect density rate of each folder was higher than our goal, leading to significant rework.

We knew that the project was deviating from the plan. This enabled us to correct the problems quickly. The test-folder development template and the associated test-folder development process were changed. The quick corrective action reduced the amount of time it took to produce subsequent folders, and we nearly met the original estimate of 768 hours. Had we not recognized early on the need to take corrective action, we would have spent the entire 768 hours producing just 19 of the 32 folders, and at that pace, we would have needed an additional 520 hours to complete the remaining folders. Imagine the painful conversation we would have had with the project's stakeholders if we had finished substantially behind schedule. Fact-based management saved us.

Controlling Change

Throughout the course of a project, change is inevitable. Management might pull resources from your project, your customer could add new requirements, technical roadblocks might crop up, or your funding might be cut. When changes happen, you must replan the project to account for them. Adjusting the plan allows it to continue to guide the work. If you don't update the plan, it soon becomes obsolete, leaving your project without the direction it needs.

Preventing change is our favorite way to use project plans to control change. By using fact-based what-if analysis, you can show that making a change to the plan is a bad business decision. For example, it is quite common for management to attempt to pull a team member from a project. Let's say that your manager asks to pull the senior designer, who is leading an effort to develop system design folders. You can use the project plan to show the manager that losing the senior designer would have negative effects on the project. Adjust the plan, remove the designer, and show the manager how the loss would affect the development of the design folders. If you can demonstrate that the designer's absence would reduce profit by three percent or delay the product to market by three months, the manager might change his or her mind.

What if management deems it appropriate to pull the person anyway? You can then use the updated plan to reset stakeholder expectations. By clearly communicating all changes to the plan, you can realign stakeholders' expectations, encourage them to commit to the updated plan, and avoid disappointing them.

You can control change by using your plan to show how new requirements would affect the project's cost and schedule. As customers learn more about the project, they almost always think of new requirements they would like to add. You can perform a what-if analysis to estimate the time and effort required to implement new requirements. Once you've told the customer how much more it will cost and how much additional time it will take to include the new requirements, the customer may decide to add the requirements and pay more or forgo them and stick with the original plan. If the requirements are added, the team would then replan the project and would share the new plan with the stakeholders to reset their expectations.

You can also use the project plan to justify adding additional resources. Let's say your project is running behind schedule on a critical path item. After conducting a what-if analysis, you realize that if you can authorize $10,000 of overtime, you will be able to prevent a two-month schedule slip, which would cost $30,000. You can use this information to convince your management team that spending an additional $10,000 in labor now will save you from spending $30,000 later.

There are many more ways you can use the project plan to control change and manage stakeholder expectations; we've shared only a few. As PMs, we have seen firsthand the benefits of updating plans and using a fact-based approach to control changes. The effort needed to keep a plan current is small compared with the value of having an up-to-date plan.

In Brief

A well-constructed, detailed plan makes it possible to complete your project efficiently, within the specified constraints, and using the requested resources. It is more than just a schedule created in Microsoft Project. The plan must help the project stakeholders understand the project's goals and the expectations and decisions that directly affect them.

A plan consists of a number of components, including a project overview, PBS, WBS, BPM, organizational structure, process definitions, and a resource-loaded schedule. With a well-constructed plan, stakeholders can identify issues very early in the schedule, which enables the PM to take corrective action immediately. This quick response allows the PM to maintain the schedule and control costs. In addition, the plan establishes a blueprint that can be used to control project deviations. A plan is one of the most important tools a PM has.

Suggested Reading and Resources

Goldratt, Eliyahu M., and Jeff Cox. *The Goal,* **2nd ed. Great Barrington, MA: The North River Press, 1992.** This business novel, which is considered very important by many, introduces the theory of constraints and emphasizes eliminating bottlenecks.

Goldratt, Eliyahu M. *Critical Chain.* **Great Barrington, MA: The North River Press, 1997.** This thought-provoking and stimulating business novel introduces readers to the author's thinking process.

O'Connell, Fergus. *How to Run Successful Projects III: The Silver Bullet,* **3rd ed. New York: Prentice Hall, 2001.** O'Connell presents ten steps of structured project management that must be taken for any project to succeed. Taking the steps, which focus primarily on project planning, will help PMs establish the conditions necessary for project success. O'Connell provides a "visualization checklist" early in the book that is meant to help PMs focus on the results of a completed project.

Pacelli, Lonnie. *The Project Management Advisor: 18 Major Screw-ups, and How to Cut Them Off at the Pass.* **Upper Saddle River, NJ: Prentice Hall, 2004.** Pacelli identifies 18 project issues—or "screw-ups"—that can be addressed or avoided by developing an effective project plan. He provides insights into why each problem happens, identifies warning signs, suggests what needs to be done, and offers specific take-aways that will help guide your planning efforts. For example, the author addresses what to do when the project lacks a good schedule, when it does not have the right sponsorship, when project team members aren't communicating effectively, and when the project team is trying to do too much.

O'Connell also addresses coping with stress. He provides a "probability of success indicator" (PSI) that, when calculated at any point in a project's life cycle, evaluates the health of the project and measures the likelihood of project success. For more information, visit the website of O'Connell's company, ETP International, at www.etpint.com.

5 Creating the Plan

Creating a plan can be an intimidating task if you've never done it before. You may find yourself defining processes you've never used before, using tools like the product breakdown structure (PBS) or work breakdown structure (WBS) for the first time, and fighting internal or external pressure to begin the project work before completing the plan. (How many times have we been encouraged by our managers to get going on "real work" and stop spending time planning?) If your project is in trouble and you're replanning it, the pressure can be even more intense. In addition to the challenges noted above, you may be fighting to overcome the negative stigma of the project's initial missteps. The project is probably already over budget and behind schedule, and many of the project's stakeholders have lost confidence in you and the team. The very existence of the project may depend on the new plan you develop and the team's ability to gain stakeholder buy-in.

How you and your team execute the process of planning or replanning sets the tone for the project as it moves forward. Your goal is to develop a realistic plan that will guide the project's work. Stakeholders, including the project team, management, and the customer, must actively participate in the plan development process (PDP) and buy into the plan for it to be effective. Without the full support of all stakeholders, it is difficult, if not impossible, to execute the plan.

The project team will most likely buy into the plan if its team leads are involved in defining and developing many of its components, including the PBS, WBS, and process definitions. The organization's management team participates in the process by tracking the plan's progress, supplying the planning resources, and signing off on the plan before delivering it to the customer. And the customer participates by tracking the plan's status, making sure that it addresses the customer's needs, assigning people to take on project responsibilities, and approving the completed plan.

Although the scope of each project is different, the process of developing the plan should be essentially the same. You will begin by developing a plan to create the plan. This plan will break the project plan development process into short-duration tasks. You'll track these tasks at the end of each day to make sure that the development of the plan is on course. You will also update stakeholders on the status of the project plan as it's developed and hold reviews to garner their buy-in. When your management and the customer formally accept the project plan and commit to supplying the resources identified in the plan, it is complete. Recognize, however, that a plan is a "living" document—it must be updated as inevitable changes to the project occur.

Defining the Plan Requirements

The project plan must meet your management's and the customer's requirements before they sign off on it, so be sure to research both parties' requirements before you even begin to write the plan. For example, if your organization mandates the use of earned-value management to track the project's performance, then the plan development team must build an earned-value tracking process into the plan. Or your customer may require that the plan itself meet certain established standards. You will find the customer's stated requirements in the contract. The team and your company are contractually obligated to meet those requirements.

Next, research any corporate policies or procedures that your organization has established. Your management team will measure your plan against these internal standards and policies before approving the plan, so it's critical that you address them. One side benefit of researching and identifying internal requirements is that you may find that your company has developed plan templates and organizational processes to make the plan development process easier.

Though meeting the stakeholders' requirements for the project plan is a major step in gaining their acceptance, sometimes that isn't enough. Some stakeholders have unspoken expectations about what they think the plan will address. To surface these unspoken expectations, the team should meet with the stakeholders to review the plan and its requirements and to explain how the plan will meet those requirements. This will give the stakeholders an opportunity to communicate any unstated requirements. If they do share new requirements for the plan, these must be addressed on a case-by-case basis. If your team thinks they are beneficial and within the scope of the project, they should be added to the PDP; if not, the new requirements should be addressed just as the team would handle other out-of-scope project requirements through the requirements management process.

Change isn't always initiated by the customer. Each project is different, and you may want to alter an approach you've used before to improve project execution. Therefore, after reviewing the internal and external plan requirements, consider whether you'd like to add additional requirements to the project plan to help you manage the project better. It's important to show the stakeholders how you intend to change the plan and to ask them to commit to these plan additions. Gaining stakeholders' buy-in before developing the plan paves the way to their accepting the plan because they will have already seen and agreed to any changes.

If the project team doesn't have a set of internal or external plan requirements, the team developing the plan should create an outline. The outline should identify all of the plan's components and briefly explain what each component will contain. Once the plan outline is complete, present it to your management team, then to the customer, for review and approval. Having the stakeholders sign off on the outline sets their expectations for what the plan will look like before you begin working on it. Also, you may find that they have valuable ideas for the plan that you hadn't considered.

Determine how much time the team will spend creating the project plan before you begin working on it. Project size, complexity, and requirements vary; the amount of time spent on planning does, too. When estimating how much time will be spent on the plan, remember that planning has two parts: the initial creation of the plan as well as time spent updating the plan as circumstances change. The total time allocated for both initial plan development and ongoing plan maintenance should total approximately ten percent of the schedule time. This means that on a one-year project, you would spend the first four weeks developing the initial project plan and then plan to spend slightly more than an additional week on maintenance. Keep in mind that some projects will require more or less planning time.

Defining the Plan Elements

In Chapter 4, we identified the major components of the project plan: the project overview, PBS and WBS, build process model (BPM), organizational structure, process definitions, and resource-loaded schedule. Because the plan must support a single vision of the project, it's logical to initiate your plan by developing the project overview, which gives the team a high-level understanding of the project's purpose that members can refer back to.

After completing the project overview, the team should then complete the PBS and WBS. The team will reference both documents during the development of the other parts of the plan. The PBS defines the products the project must create. (The PBS development process is covered in detail in Chapter 7.)

After completing the PBS, the team should develop the WBS. The WBS identifies all of the work to be done on the project. This includes work needed to produce every product in the PBS as well as work required to support the project that doesn't directly lead to the creation of a product, such as project management or technical leadership. (The WBS development process is covered in detail in Chapter 8.)

After completing the PBS and WBS, the team should develop the build process model (BPM; Figure 5-1). The BPM identifies all of the project's work processes, including the inputs and outputs of each process. For example, on a construction project, there might be a process to develop building plans. The building plans are an input to the site survey, another work process. The product of the site survey process is a surveyed site, which is an input to the excavation process, and so on. The BPM establishes the relationships between processes, which helps the team develop a common understanding of them.

After completing the BPM, the PM has a detailed understanding of all of the products that must be produced, all of the work that must be accomplished, and the relationship that exists between the work processes. The PM can then develop an organizational structure to support the execution of the work. First, the PM defines the roles and responsibilities

FIGURE 5-1: Build Process Model

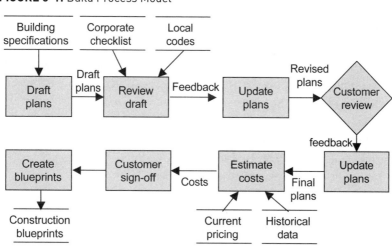

The phrases in between the boxed tasks are work products, and the outlined phrases are inputs.

Defining tasks and dependencies helps team members understand how each task will be accomplished. The arrows in the graphic indicate dependencies.

of each member of the organizational structure, providing each a clear understanding of what he or she must do.

As the PM develops the organizational structure, the rest of the planning team can define the detailed process elements identified in the BPM. The BPM for the construction project mentioned previously might list a process for developing building plans. In the relevant section of the project plan, the team would define the details of the process of creating the building plans. Doing this helps the project team understand how to take the construction requirements and convert them into a set of blueprints. Creating a detailed process will also help set your stakeholders' expectations for the work to be done and their roles in the process. For example, a building-plans process would tell your management team to have a team of architects available to review the draft plans before customer delivery. It would also state that the customer must review and sign off on the draft set of plans before the blueprints are created.

Processes usually fall into one of three categories: management, engineering, or support. Management processes include risk management, subcontractor management, and communication planning. Engineering processes are those process used to create the product, such as the design, development, and testing processes. Support processes include defect prevention—identifying the root causes of an existing problem to prevent another problem in the future—and configuration management—strictly controlling changes to documentation, hardware, software, and other products. When planning the project plan, the team must identify all of the processes that will be used so that the development of these processes can be built into the plan for the project plan.

Project Activity Types

Figure 5-2 indicates the appropriate proportions of the three general types of project activities. Your plan must account for configuration management, defect prevention, and quality assurance/quality control, in particular. These must be carefully analyzed and documented in the WBS and in the project plan.

FIGURE 5-2: Project Activity Types

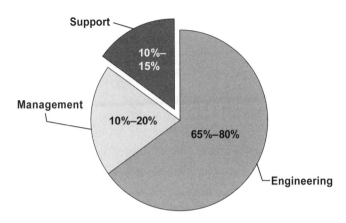

- *Management activities* include establishing supplier agreements (including subcontractors' relationships), defining metrics and data collection procedures, defining and managing risks, managing customer change, and communicating with stakeholders.

- *Engineering activities* include establishing a development environment, acquiring equipment and tools, and defining product life cycle processes, including requirements development, design, construction, reviews, verification, and validation.

- *Support activities* include establishing configuration management (CM) processes and a CM environment, establishing quality assurance/quality control (QA/QC) procedures, establishing an effective defect-prevention process, and reviewing lessons learned from prior similar projects. Too often, project teams consider management and engineering activities, but they may underbid their budget or schedule by 10–15 percent by not addressing the support activities.

Applicability of Planning Activities

As was emphasized earlier in the book, too often on projects we just "do" without planning. The problem with this approach is that it results in a lot of rework. It is fraught with errors, and it doesn't consider related activities in advance of doing the work. A good PM budgets for some rework, but he or she also expects that the developers will deliver high-quality products. Rework, especially late in the project life cycle, is a leading cause of missed deadlines and overspending.

It's important to understand that any process or activity can be *scaled* (reduced or increased in size and scope as required for a particular use) or *tailored* (changed to make it appropriate for a particular need or application). For example, performing QA on a project can add a lot of value if it verifies that the documented process is actually being used and identifies recommendations for continuous improvement of the processes and procedures. Figure 5-3 highlights how planning activities can be tailored for a smaller project.[1]

How to Write a Section of a Plan

When preparing to write part of the project plan, choose a writer with experience doing the work activities he or she is about to document. The writer should review plans used on previous projects, then identify the relevant people or project team organizations and invite them to participate in the development of the plan. Their involvement is critical because they must have a sense of ownership and be committed to using the plan for

FIGURE 5-3: Tailoring a Project Plan for Smaller Projects

Planning Tasks: Larger Project	Planning Tasks: Smaller Project
Initiation meeting	Initiation meeting
Identify staff	Identify staff
Subcontractor agreements	
Identify products (PBS)	Identify products (PBS)
Plan work environment	Plan work environment
Identify office space, furniture, etc.	
Define integration/test environment	Define integration/test environment
Perform initial risk assessments	Perform initial risk assessments
Determine quality assurance needs	

it to succeed. Try using simple flow charts to define and document work during plan development—these are often easier to follow than verbal descriptions of required activities and actions.

Planning Using Inch Stones[2]

Creating a plan for developing the project plan is similar to executing the project; it's all about breaking the work into smaller, more manageable pieces. The most effective way to define and track a project plan's development is to split the development work into units that will take hours, not days or weeks, to complete.

We've dubbed these small tasks *inch stones*. Inch stones define work at a detailed level so that progress, or lack thereof, can be ascertained quickly. This approach facilitates prompt action or replanning if progress is not being made. It's essential that the team complete the plan's components by the stated due dates. As the team meets the due date for each inch stone, it will gain confidence, and the project's stakeholders will gain confidence in the team.

If you keep each plan development task to a duration of approximately one day, you will know at the end of each day if you've met your target. If you haven't, you can take corrective action immediately. Remember, it is significantly easier to make small adjustments than it is to make major corrections.

Using inch stones enables you to use fact-based earned-value techniques, rather than subjective techniques, to determine how much work has been completed. (We recommend that you examine earned-value techniques in more detail. There are entire books on tracking earned value, such as Paul J. Solomon and Ralph R. Young's *Performance-Based Earned Value*.[3]) Fact-based techniques provide a far more accurate assessment of the work that has actually been done than do techniques such as percent complete, in which a team is assumed to be halfway done with its plan if it has expended half of its planned hours, even if the team is not really making progress.

To track the development progress of the plan using *milestone weighting,* a fact-based technique, assume that a completed project plan is worth 100 percent. Each inch stone leading to the development of the plan is worth some portion of that 100 percent. Figure 5-4 is an example of how we might distribute the value among the inch stones. The larger the inch stone, the greater the value it is assigned.

FIGURE 5-4: Weighting Milestones

Section of the Plan	Value
Project overview	4 percent
Product breakdown structure	10 percent
Work breakdown structure	10 percent
Project organizational structure	5 percent
Build process model	5 percent
Process definitions	26 processes worth two percent each
Resource-loaded schedule	14 percent

After you complete a scheduled inch stone, you have finished the corresponding percentage of the plan. At the end of each day, you will note the inch stones that have been completed, allowing you to quickly and easily calculate the status of the plan.

To communicate to stakeholders the status of the plan's development, simply identify the completed tasks and take credit for the percentage of work completed. If the team has completed the project overview (worth 4 percent), the PBS (10 percent), and the WBS (10 percent), the plan is 24 percent complete. Using this technique to track and communicate progress removes much of the subjectivity from taking credit for work completed. You are either done with a task or you are not. The objectivity and accuracy of milestone weighting helps convince project stakeholders that you can develop a plan and stick to it.

Monitoring and Communicating Plan Development Status

To maximize the benefits of creating a detailed plan, you must monitor it and regularly communicate its development status to certain groups: the plan development team, the team's internal management, and the project's external stakeholders.

At the end of each day, plan development team members should update the PM on the status of the day's inch stones, and the PM should verify completion of each. This shows the team that the PM holds members accountable for their work, encouraging them to focus on completing the task at hand. Every few days, the PM should convene the team to discuss the status of the plan. These meetings are great opportunities to solicit improvement ideas, identify potential problems, and recognize good work.

Breaking work down into inch stones, accountability, and tracking progress are concepts the team will carry forward to the project after the plan is complete. Using this approach to create the plan gives the PM and the team experience in working this way and imparts confidence that the project as a whole can be executed like this.

You should meet with internal management once a week during the planning process. The management team is interested in cost and schedule performance, so you should provide it with overviews of the week's objectives, your progress toward them, any corrective actions taken, resource needs, and the tasks scheduled for the following week.

Because you have divided the planning process into milestone-weighted inch stones, you'll be able to easily provide management with quantitative information about the plan's status. For example, at the end of the first week, if you planned to complete the first three scheduled tasks, each with a milestone weight of 4 percent, and you were able to complete all three, you can report that you are on schedule and that you have completed 12 percent of the overall plan.

If the team completed only two of the first three tasks, you can tell management that you planned to have completed 12 percent of the plan, but you have actually completed 8 percent. If the unfinished task will take one day, you can report that you are one day behind schedule and explain what you are doing to get back on track. In our experience, if you accurately present the data to management and proactively correct any problems, you will soon gain their confidence.

Weekly meetings with external stakeholders will be similar to those you'll have with internal management. You'll report on the week's objectives, your progress toward those objectives, any corrective actions taken, and an overview of the tasks scheduled for the following week. But there are two additional topics that you should cover. If the external stakeholders have been charged with tasks to support plan development, they should review them and give status updates. Doing so reminds the stakeholders that they, too, are accountable for their commitments.

You should also provide a high-level overview of what the plan currently looks like. This will help set the stakeholders' expectations of what the final product will contain and shows them that tangible progress is being made toward its completion. Do not give the stakeholders a copy of the incomplete work; instead, tell them that the plan must go through a release process to ensure quality before it can be delivered to outside parties. This will prevent the stakeholders from judging the plan's quality before it has undergone the proper reviews.

In Brief

Even if you have prior experience, creating a plan can be very challenging. It's critical to obtain stakeholder acceptance during the planning process. Without stakeholder support, it becomes difficult, if not impossible, to execute the plan. Techniques for gaining stakeholders' approval during plan development include soliciting their input and holding regular meetings to keep them informed. Developing a plan should be considered a mini-project with its own schedule and resources. We recommend building the plan using a series of very small, manageable tasks called inch stones that help you monitor progress. This progress must be tracked and frequently reported to the stakeholders. Your objective is to create a completed plan approved by *all* stakeholders, including your management and the customer.

Suggested Reading and Resources

Brooks, Frederick P., Jr. *The Mythical Man-Month.* **Reading, MA: Addison-Wesley, 1995.** In this oft-cited software project management book, first published in 1975, the author draws from his experience as a PM at IBM to assess software engineering and programming. Brooks' principal assertion is that adding more man-power to troubled software projects will not help the situation; rather, it will hinder the project further because the new team members will have to learn about the project and will require more overhead communication to coordinate efforts.

Martin, Paula and Karen G. Tate. *Project Management Memory Jogger™: A Pocket Guide for Project Teams.* **Salem, NH: GOAL/QPC, 1997.** This is one of a series of pocket guides written by various industry experts and published by GOAL/QPC (www.goal/qpc.com), a leading provider of books, tools, and other resources for project and organizational improvement. A lengthy portion of this book addresses how to create a project plan. The authors identify nine categories of activities that are needed to create a project plan—i.e., what you need to do to accomplish a step of the project planning process, when you need to do it, and how to do it. They emphasize the need to create quality criteria and assess risks, bring the right people to the team, create a project schedule, create an activity schedule and a Gantt Chart, make resource estimates, and create a project budget.

Tsui, Frank. *Managing Software Projects.* **Sudbury, MA: Jones and Bartlett Publishers, 2004.** This book targets software PMs and emphasizes project planning by providing a detailed description of task analysis, including a comprehensive explanation of how to use a WBS to analyze tasks and how to assign resources to tasks. The book also includes a detailed discussion of project resource planning for three types of resources—human resources, processes and methodologies, and tools and equipment—as well as an example of a project change control process.

Notes

1. There is no industry agreement on the definition of a "small project." One could consider it a "team." Often it is considered a project involving one to six professionals operating for as long as three to six months, but this definition is arbitrary. Consideration has been given in the industry literature to whether "small projects" are really all that different from "medium-size" or even "large" projects. . . . Members of small projects should be encouraged to take what they can from the experiences of larger projects by tailoring the approach, rather than using smallness as an excuse for not taking advantage of industry lessons. For a perspective giving careful attention and focus to "smallness," see Brodman and Johnson, *The LOGOS Tailored CMM for Small Businesses, Small Organizations, and Small Projects*. The changes tailor the Capability Maturity Model® for Software (SW-CMM) for a small project environment. Participants in small projects or organizations may find this reference helpful. (From Young, *Effective Requirements Practices*, the entire footnote on pp. 58, Copyright © 2001 Addison Wesley. Reproduced by permission of Pearson Education, Inc.)

2. Industry references cite three originators of the term *inch pebbles,* also known as *inch stones* or *miniature milestones*: Fred Brooks, in his book *The Mythical Man Month* (although Brooks does not take credit for the concept); the Software Program Managers Network (SPMN)—see Norm Brown, "Industrial-Strength Measurement Strategies"; and Tom DeMarco. Norm Brown characterizes inch pebbles as a best practice, as does Steve McConnell in his book *Rapid Development: Taming Wild Software Schedules*. A good description of the concept is also provided in Johanna Rothman, "How to Use Inch-Pebbles When You Think You Can't." An extensive treatment of binary quality gates at the inch-pebble level is provided on the DACS Gold Practices website, www.goldpractices.com/practices/bqg/index.php.

    One project management expert and former process engineer at SPMN, John E. Moore, wrote in a 2009 email to Ralph Young that he believes that planning and tracking work at a low and short-term level is a noble goal, but it is useful only on projects where the development team is familiar with the concept of inch pebbles and has used them before. For challenging projects that are unfamiliar to development teams, however, planning at the inch-pebble level tends not to provide any real benefit and in fact can be counter-productive.

    Mark Paulk disagrees with Moore. In a 2009 email to Ralph Young, Paulk wrote that he bases this opinion on the fact that all "user stories in the agile methods satisfy the definition of an inch pebble. You just can't plan at that level of detail more than a couple of months out; the agile methods make that explicit. So to the degree that you think agile methods have a useful place in the constellation of software engineering methods, you'll see some real benefit to the idea [of inch pebbles], even if the terminology is different."

3. A synopsis of *Performance-Based Earned Value* is provided at the end of Chapter 2.

6 Building a Team

Building the right team is critical to the success of executing the project plan. As a PM, you could create the greatest plan in the world, but if your team is not capable of executing the plan, you will not succeed. What would happen if a football coach built a great game plan—but asked a high school team to execute it against an NFL championship team? Even with a solid plan and intense effort, the high school players could not compete against a professional team. To build a strong project team, you have to recruit the right talent, create a unified vision, set expectations, and tell the stakeholders how the team will function.

The best results are produced not by the heroic efforts of a few individuals acting alone, but when the entire team works together. Your team as a whole must be able to fulfill all of the roles and responsibilities mandated by the plan. Building a team with the right mix of skills requires looking beyond each member's technical skills. You must make sure that the team has leadership skills, too. PMs rely heavily on the project's team leads to help execute the plan. These team leads are extensions of the PM and work together with him or her to make sure that their sub-teams make progress each day. The team leads help the sub-teams stay focused on the team's vision.

Your team's cultural norms are influenced by how the team carries out the plan and adheres to its vision. PMs can create and maintain a vision by making sure that everyone on the team understands the project's mission, the products to be created, each member's role, and the team's defined processes. Establishing a vision begins during the planning phase, and the vision must be reinforced throughout the life of the project. As we discussed in Chapter 5, the PM should hold weekly team meetings to review the plan, track team performance, and adjust the plan so it continues to guide the work. These actions help keep the team's focus in line with the project vision.

As the PM, you must ensure that each individual contributor understands his or her role and what is expected of him or her. Each team member's actions must support the team's vision and objectives so that the team can work together efficiently toward meeting the same goals. When selecting team members, look at the personality of each individual to make sure that he or she is capable of working in a team environment. Everyone on the team must follow the team's processes. Nothing damages team cohesiveness more than individuals who disregard team processes. Other team members will wonder why they have to adhere to standards their colleagues ignore.

Stakeholders, including the customer and your company's management, or other employees can be a source of distraction. Let's say one of your company's managers asks a member of your team to help solve a problem on a project she worked on previously. She agrees, assuming that it won't take long to help out, but the "minor request" ends up taking days, and she is unable to finish an inch stone on your project. PMs rarely spend enough time thinking about protecting the team from such distractions. If requests like these aren't managed and communicated through the proper channels, they can harm your project. You must explain to external stakeholders, and, of course, your team, how the team is structured and how special requests should be handled.

Defining the Team Composition

Before you select team members, you must create the organizational structure, including defining members' roles and responsibilities. You'll define these roles and responsibilities after creating both the product breakdown structure (PBS) and the work breakdown structure (WBS).

The PBS and WBS, respectively, define all the products and work to be accomplished during the execution of the project. These detailed planning products must be complete before you select your team so that you can choose individuals with the right skills.

If you do not define roles and responsibilities before selecting your team, you'll likely create an unbalanced team composed of too many people with the same set of skills and not enough people with other required skills. You might, for example, select individuals who have great technical talent, but forget to consider the project's big-picture needs. Let's say you're managing a home construction project. You haven't defined roles and responsibilities for the project, but you know that you need carpenters, masons, roofers, and other technically skilled people on your team. But when the time comes to frame the house, you realize that you've hired only finish carpenters who have never done framing work. You could ask your carpenters to do the framing, but they would take longer to frame the house and would probably make more mistakes than would skilled framers. You would face rework, additional costs, and schedule slips. Or you could stop the work to hire carpenters who have the skills you need—which also would put the project behind schedule. Both options would hurt your project.

Try to build a team consisting of members with complementary skills. If your team is charged with developing a web-based software application and writing technical documentation, you would look for programmers good at developing database code, others who are skilled in designing and developing web-based screens, and some who excel at writing technical documentation. You might choose an exceptional developer who doesn't write well and pair him or her with another developer who is a good writer but might not have strong development skills.

The team leaders you select should be well-balanced, possessing diverse sets of skills and the ability to comfortably shift between different project situations: solving technical problems, briefing management and customers, managing team members, and, of course, doing technical work. A common mistake is designating the team's best technical person as a leader. If he or she lacks the necessary leadership skills, his or her sub-team's part of the project could be in jeopardy.

Let's say that you've selected your team's best technician as the project's technical lead. She enjoys the technical aspects of her job but doesn't like giving presentations. You've asked her to present the product's design to the customer during the critical design review. If her presentation is poor, the customer might mistakenly consider it an indicator of the quality of the designs and refuse to approve them, bringing the project to a halt.

You should not consider the initial cost of prospective team members as the driving factor in deciding who to select. Although cost is always an important consideration, do not look solely at the hourly cost of each individual. Consider the total project cost when making these decisions because the more expensive resource may be able to complete the work faster and cheaper. Also, do not hesitate to leave positions vacant rather than filling them with the wrong people. Selecting the wrong person almost always leads to rework. In the long run, recruiting "less expensive" individuals or ineffective ones will cost the project more.

Let's say that two people are candidates for a vacancy on your team. One costs $20 an hour, the other $25 an hour. The less expensive candidate would save you $10,400 a year in labor costs, all other factors being equal. But if this candidate produces unacceptable work, the savings will turn into a project expense. You will have to pay another person to correctly redo the work and will end up spending about twice as much as you would have if you had selected the more expensive candidate. It is cheaper in the end to wait until the right person is available. You may feel pressured to select someone else so you can save money or begin the work sooner, but for the sake of your project, you must resist that pressure.

Creating the Team Vision

Once you have selected your team, you must share the team's vision with its members. The vision is created during the project's planning process and is maintained throughout the life of the project. Your goal is to focus the team on the finish line and on taking the same path to the finish line. The PBS and WBS set the finish line; the path is established in the project plan.

To communicate the vision, connect the specific work the team will do to the mission or charter of the project, which explains why the project was initiated and the purpose it will serve. Tie the team's assigned inch stones to the products and work to underscore their importance and explain how the work will help the team achieve its collective goals.

Team members must understand how the processes established in the plan will help them perform the work better than they could without the processes. To reinforce the value of following the processes, you must shift the way you reward performance. As the PM, you have to look for ways to reward the team initially for following the processes. After members become comfortable with the processes, you should reward them for finding ways to improve them. If you simply reward employees for completing inch stones but don't verify that they followed the relevant process, you might undermine the plan. If you reward individuals who ignored the team's processes, you send a message to the rest of the team that they can disregard the plan. If the team disregards the plan, you will quickly lose control of the project. But if you reward the team for following and improving processes, everyone will benefit.

One of the most important benefits of having a single vision and established team processes is that the team's work—both the time it takes and the quality of the products—becomes predictable. Because everyone on the team is using the same processes, you can track the time it takes to execute the processes, then use the data to predict future work or make adjustments to the plan. In Chapter 8, we discuss in detail how work estimates are created for the WBS and how those are then incorporated into the plan. The most accurate predictor of a team's future work is its historical performance. Naturally, using the most accurate method of predicting project work will lead to increasingly accurate plans.

Tracking the completion of the project's products and analyzing the defect data during project execution enables you to establish quality standards for the products. Using these quality standards, you can improve the team's processes and thereby improve product quality. You'll also be able to predict the quality of future products the team creates. This will improve your planning. You will be able to plan how much time will be needed to correct defects and predict whether the product's quality will meet the customer's acceptance criteria.

The PM has the authority to enforce project processes. He or she can exert this type of control during the product release authorization (PRA) process. We execute this process on our projects before delivering any product. It calls for the project's quality assurance officer, the configuration manager, the product's producer, the PM and the line manager responsible for the project to convene to review the product's quality and configuration data before delivery. In the PRA meeting, the team confirms that the product was made using the team's processes, the product was reviewed and defects were corrected, and the product met all of the project's standards. The PM can prevent delivery if all of these conditions have not been met. This makes clear to the team that following the processes is mandatory and quality is essential.

Setting the Team's Expectations

After creating a vision for the team, you must explain how you expect it to fulfill the vision. At the beginning of the project, make sure that every team member fully understands his or her role on the project, the plan, and what you expect from the team as a whole.

First, the PM must identify and define the role of each team member. Hold a one-on-one meeting with each person. Explain his or her role and duties and the standards to which all team members must adhere. Give each member a copy of the team's organizational structure and a document detailing the roles of everyone on the team. These meetings give each team member the chance to ask questions about his or her role and the organizational structure, which will reduce the risk of confusion about project roles and responsibilities. If the team size is manageable, the PM should meet with each member. If it's a very large team, each sub-team lead should meet with every member of his or her sub-team.

After conducting the role assignment meetings, convene the team. In this meeting, give the team a detailed briefing of the project plan, explain what is expected from members in their interactions with each other, and define for them your vision for the type of team they will be. This meeting helps establish the team's culture.

Also during the initial team meeting, begin setting behavioral expectations. What should team members do if, for example, a project stakeholder requests out-of-scope work or ignores a team process? They must tell the stakeholder that there is a defined team process for submitting requests, then explain how to follow the process. Make clear that these processes exist to help the project team control difficult situations and that they will help the team stay on task. Also establish team standards at the beginning of the project. These might include, for example, taking minutes at each meeting.

Most people dislike having their mistakes pointed out to them and may even try to hide mistakes from others. This is detrimental to a project, so at the beginning of the project, you must acknowledge that mistakes are inevitable. One of the team's most important duties is to find and fix defects before delivering products to the customer, so admitting mistakes actually benefits the project.

As a PM, you must lead by example. Follow all team processes and standards, and reward the team for doing the same. If you are not committed to the plan and the team's processes, your team won't be, either. But if you follow the processes and the team can see their value, the team will discipline itself. This makes your job easier; you'll spend less time policing the team and more time managing the project.

Communicating with Stakeholders

Controlling stakeholders' interactions with the team and purposefully shaping their view of the project's vision will help you execute the project plan. When you meet with each set of stakeholders to explain the team's vision, you must address each group's unique needs and interests. You'll also review and agree on each group's role on the project, define communication processes, and discuss other relevant processes.

When you meet with your customer, for example, you will review the PRA process that the team will execute before delivering each product. Explain that you will withhold delivery of a product if it doesn't meet your team's quality standards. Make sure the customer understands that the process helps ensure product quality. Also at this meeting, you should review the process for introducing new project requirements. Explain that any new requirements will first be analyzed for cost and schedule impacts and that principal stakeholders—e.g., the project team PM, customer PM, and project sponsor—will have to approve them before they are incorporated. If in the future a stakeholder tries to introduce additional requirements outside the set process, the team can remind the stakeholder of the process (and of the meeting in which it was discussed).

Setting the stakeholders' expectations early makes handling difficult situations easier. Let's say that that a deliverable did not meet your release standards. It is easier to explain the delay in delivery to the customer if you can relate it to the PRA process you've already discussed. Most customers appreciate this attention to quality and would rather receive a high-quality product slightly late than a poor-quality product on time.

The vision and expectations initially established with your stakeholders must be reinforced throughout the life of the project. In Chapter 11, we cover the management of stakeholder expectations and provide a detailed approach to managing these expectations through regularly scheduled status meetings. Remember, you and your team must follow the established processes and procedures if you want your stakeholders to follow suit. Doing so will help your project run much more smoothly, and you will be better able to keep the stakeholders focused on the same vision as your team.

In Brief

You must assemble a team capable of executing your project plan, or your project will fail. Complete your team's organizational structure, including defining the roles and responsibilities of its members, before selecting team members. You should focus on choosing a team with not only the right mix of technical skills but also the right mix of leadership skills. Team leaders help the PM ensure that daily tasks are executed, so it is essential that they have strong leadership ability. Each team member must understand his or her roles and responsibilities as outlined in the plan in order to do his or her job properly and work toward project success. Finally, it's imperative that the PM lead by example, following all team processes and standards. This encourages team members and stakeholders to do the same.

Suggested Reading and Resources

Burlton, Roger T. *Business Process Management: Profiting from Process.* **Indianapolis, ID: Sams Publishing, 2001.** Business process management (BPM) is an approach enterprises can use to make their organizations survive and thrive. Through processes, people must use technologies, facilities, information, and knowledge to support enterprise outcomes that deliver value to the organization's stakeholders. The author elaborates on ten straightforward principles of process management that focus on delivering business results to customers and satisfying the needs of the organization's other stakeholders. The book also includes a process management framework based on best practices in the profession of business change management. Additional topics include project requirements, project planning, and implementing new processes.

Humphrey, Watts S. *Introduction to the Team Software Process.* **Reading, MA: Addison-Wesley, 2000.** Humphrey is a superb writer, and here he shares his tremendous insight into what makes software teams work effectively. Though this book is focused on software development projects, it's a valuable resource for anyone seeking to improve team effectiveness.

Humphrey explains how to implement strategies that facilitate good work, including:

- Eliminating work that gets in the way of improving the product

- Systematically tracking project progress

- Creating an environment that fosters unbridled enthusiasm

- Using milestone scheduling to keep schedules aggressive but not unrealistic

- Focusing on personal growth goals as well as necessary work

- Promoting beneficial attitudes, such as a continuous improvement ethic.

Humphrey, Watts S. *Winning With Software: An Executive Strategy.* Reading, MA: Addison-Wesley, 2002. This book underscores the benefits of developing a software development team and provides methods for doing so. The book targets software executives, but the same techniques for building and measuring team performance can be applied across functional disciplines.

Paulk, Mark C. "The 'Soft Side' of Software Process Improvement." Pittsburgh, PA: Software Engineering Institute, Carnegie Mellon University. Presentation, December 1999. Paulk is the leading author of the Capability Maturity Model® for Software (SW-CMM) and has deep sensitivity to the people-related aspects of the industry. Several valuable insights are presented in this briefing: 1) the most capable people outperform the least capable by approximately ten to one; 2) the best performer is 2.5 times more productive than the median performer; 3) organizations operating at CMM levels 4 and 5 tend to have required training in team-building, negotiation skills, interpersonal skills, domain knowledge, management skills, and technical skills; and 4) people tend to be overly optimistic about their abilities.

Scholtes, Peter R., Brian L. Joiner, and Barbara J. Streibel. *The Team Handbook,* 2nd ed. Madison, WI: Oriel, 2001. To succeed in today's environment, the authors argue, the knowledge, skills, experience, and perspectives of a wide range of people must be brought together. This book describes how to start a quality initiative, offers strategies for leading change, and provides advice on delivering an effective presentation. It also provides concise descriptions of quality tools, including affinity diagrams, prioritization matrices, effort/impact grids, and planning tools, and it discusses how to identify and control process variation. Other topics covered that will benefit PMs in particular include leadership, organizational development, and the dynamics of a team-based environment.

Walton, Mary. T*he Deming Management Method.* New York: The Putnam Publishing Group, 1986. This is a good summary and explanation of Dr. W. Edward Deming's teachings, particularly his "Fourteen Points," "Seven Deadly Diseases," and "Parable of the Red Beads." Dr. Deming believed that management is the primary cause of the results in organizations. He challenged managers to recognize the distinction between a stable system and an unstable one and to recognize and address special causes. He also described the conditions necessary to achieve teamwork. This book will be especially valuable to anyone seeking a good understanding of quality improvement.

7 Identifying the Products

This chapter will help you identify all of your project's products. You will then be able to build a plan that takes into account all of the work required to create these products. A *product* is any tangible thing that must be created to complete a task. Products may be physical structures, such as buildings; paper-based, such as reports, designs, or plans; or electronic, such as lines of software code.

The purpose of the plan is to guide the project, so you must identify *all* of the products to be produced during the plan development process (PDP) so that the plan can be built to guide *all* of the needed work. If a project team does not identify all of the products it must build, it cannot account for all the associated work or accurately estimate the effort, time, and resources required to execute the project effectively. If the plan does not address all of the needed resources or allow enough time to get the job done, then the project automatically starts behind schedule and over budget. Underestimating the effort needed is a major reason projects get into trouble. To minimize this risk, we recommend that you develop a product breakdown structure (PBS).

The development of a comprehensive PBS is a critical step in the success of the PDP. The PBS answers the question "What will this project produce?" We've managed projects of all different sizes, and no matter the size, the process we went through to develop the PBS for each was surprisingly similar to that for the others and equally effective.

The Purpose of the PBS

The concept behind the PBS is simple: identify all of the things that need to be produced. Project team members are usually adept at quickly identifying the products related to their own areas of expertise. For example, if a project's charter is designing, developing, and building a new city park, the project team will consist of playground designers, managers, tradespeople, and others.

The playground designers will identify their products, such as the plans for the playground. The tradespeople know that their products are constructed pieces of equipment—swing sets, park benches, shelters, and water fountains. But what about products that aren't so obvious? These might include monthly progress reports submitted to the city council, monthly budget analyses, news releases to the public, and completed permit applications.

Some team members may not care about the products their teammates produce. But if certain products are not accounted for in the project plan, the resulting schedule and budget overruns will affect all parts of the project and all members of the team. Also, there may be direct relationships between products. For example, the team may have to acquire a permit before the tradespeople can begin construction work. That's why it is important to explain the relationships between products to the team. Each group of specialists on your team will look at the project from a different perspective and will be charged with differing tasks, but all of them must work together to create an effective plan.

Identifying all of the products to be built is only the first step in creating a PBS. Figure 7-1 highlights the three purposes of the PBS process: identifying all of the products to be built, estimating their respective sizes, and defining appropriate quality objectives. For the PBS to effectively prevent the project from starting behind schedule and over budget, the team must accurately estimate product size and carefully document quality requirements. A comprehensive PBS helps the team determine project personnel and time needs.

FIGURE 7-1: Identifying the Products

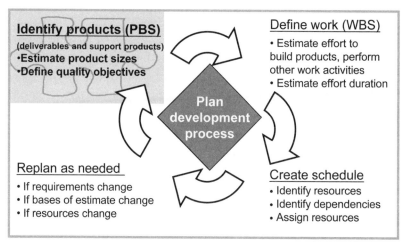

Consider the difference in work associated with developing a 5-acre city park versus developing a 100-acre park. The project, building a park, is the same, but the effort required to build each park is substantially different and must be taken into account when planning.

Now consider how poor product quality would affect the park project. If the initial set of plans developed for the park was rejected by the city's engineers, the team would have to revise the plans and resubmit them for the engineers' review before the park could break ground. The project plan likely would not have accounted for this extra work, which would delay the schedule.

Preparing to Build the PBS

The PBS can be created quickly using a relatively simple process, and the use of existing project artifacts (documents) facilitates its development. A project team can develop a PBS for a small project in less than a day; for a large project, in a couple of days. Proper preparation for PBS creation is critical to the efficiency and effectiveness of the process. Make sure that the project team has all of the information it needs to build the document. Preparing for the PBS meeting is simple: Collect existing project artifacts, identify team members to participate in the process, and have the necessary resources in place.

The first step is to collect project information. Prepare copies of the contract and the corresponding statement of work (SOW)[1] for team members to reference. These documents define many of the project deliverables, so team members must consult them as they build the PBS. If they do not, they could forget to include a key deliverable in the PBS. If a key contract deliverable is missed at this stage, you might put yourself at risk of breach of contract and subject the project to legal challenges—in addition to starting behind schedule and over budget.

In addition to the products listed in the contract and statement of work, identify any necessary internal products, such as internal status or budget reports. Status and budget reports are typically developed by the project team, but they are routinely overlooked in the planning process because they are not identified in the contract. These internal products are typically mandated by internal organizational standards and therefore must be included in the project plan.

Another resource in developing a PBS is historical data from previous projects. The products produced on similar projects may indicate the need for those same products on your current project. Analyze previous projects completed by the organization, and identify those that best align with the size and scope of the current project. Returning to the example of the city park project, the team should review the products created in support of previous park-building projects to identify relevant products for the current project. Analyze the size of the products and how long it took to build them. This kind of historical review will help minimize the risk of forgetting a key product and will provide a solid basis of estimate.

Next, you must select the right team to build the PBS. Every group on the project team—such as planners, designers, engineers, and tradespeople—should be represented. The number of team members needed to produce a PBS varies greatly depending on the size of the project. On a large-scale project, it is common to bring in a representative for each project area. If there are 20 tradespeople on the team, choose one or two to represent the group. You might include a foreman who is very familiar with the work to be done, has helped create PBSs for previous projects, and will be responsible for overseeing the work and making sure it is done properly. The foreman has a vested interest in identifying and planning for his or her group's work because the foreman's personal performance will be evaluated based on the group's. On a small-scale project, a single individual may represent the interests of several different project groups. For example, on a small software development project, the technical lead may represent the software designers and developers.

Finally, make practical preparations for the PBS development meeting. First, select a meeting space. Make sure the meeting room is large enough to comfortably hold the PBS development team and will facilitate uninterrupted work. Then gather necessary supplies such as Post-it® notes, markers, computers, and perhaps a projector.

Developing the PBS and Defining the Products

Having conducted more than 50 PBS meetings, we've found that the best way to start identifying products is to list all of the project deliverables named in the contract and the corresponding statement of work. Begin with the contract because of the critical nature of the products it lists. Starting with the contract also helps team members ease into the PBS process because it explicitly states the products to be made.

Products typically fall into one of two groups: management or technical. *Management products* are those associated with managing the project, and *technical products* are created in support of project development. The management and technical product groups can be split into sub-groups of internal and external products. *External products* will be delivered to the customer. *Internal products* will never be seen by the customer, but are nonetheless critical. These may include internal status-meeting presentations or technical processes and procedures. Write the name of each sub-group on a Post-it® note or larger piece of paper, and stick them to the wall.

Then create a category under each of the four existing product sub-groups (external management, internal management, external technical, and internal technical) for each project area, such as design, engineering, and testing. Use a Post-it® note or sheet of paper stuck to the wall to designate these categories, too.

The PBS development team then collaborates to determine which products fall under each category. As you identify each product, write its name on a Post-it® note, one product per note. Adhere each note to the wall under the appropriate heading.

When you are confident that all of the products have been identified, document the PBS. Spreadsheets work very well for this. Note the product's name and assign a unique number to each one. Later, you'll include additional data about each product, such as the unit of measure to be used, estimated size, and quality objectives. This data will be used as an input to the work breakdown structure (WBS; covered in Chapter 8) and the project schedule (discussed in Chapter 9). Figure 7-2 summarizes this approach, noting examples of products in each of the four categories specified above.

FIGURE 7-2: Categorizing Products

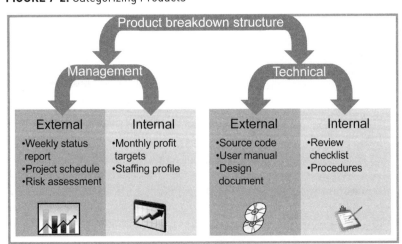

Figure 7-3 shows a partial sample PBS. Note the headings in the template. The products are listed within the four categories, and the estimated size and units of measure are provided.

FIGURE 7-3: PBS Template

PBS #	Product	Technical/Management	Size	Unit	...
1.0	**Management products**	Management			...
1.1	PBS	Internal management	100	items	...
1.2	WBS	Internal management	200	items	...
1.3	Master schedule	External management	80	tasks	...
1.4	Status reports	External management	28	pages	...
2.0	**Technical products**	Technical			...
2.1	Storyboard	Internal technical	85	slides	...
2.2	Draft	External technical	192	pages	...
2.2.1	Draft of Chapter 1	External technical	12	pages	...
2.2.2	Draft of Chapter 2	External technical	12	pages	...

Estimating Product Size

After identifying the products, the next step in building the PBS is to estimate the product size (Figure 7-4).

FIGURE 7-4: Estimating Product Size and Effort

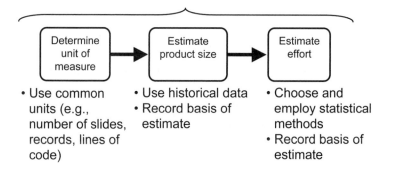

Estimate size before effort

Determine unit of measure	Estimate product size	Estimate effort
• Use common units (e.g., number of slides, records, lines of code)	• Use historical data • Record basis of estimate	• Choose and employ statistical methods • Record basis of estimate

To estimate the size of each product, it's important to:

- Establish a consistent unit of measure
- Use historical data when possible
- Record the basis of estimate—the reasoning behind the estimate
- Track the actual size against the estimated size throughout the life of the project.

The unit of measure you will use depends on the product. A house might be measured in square feet, and a computer program might be measured in lines of code. Remember to make sure the unit of measure has a defined standard that can be reused for a similar product of the same type. For example, let's say the unit of measurement for a document is the number of pages. Though this seems like an easy unit of measure to count and track, the data can be very misleading without standards. Let's say that one team member produces a 10-page single-spaced document using a 10-point font with half-inch margins on the top, bottom, and sides. Another team member creates a 10-page double-spaced document using a 12-point font with one-inch margins on the top, bottom, and sides. Even though the documents are both 10 pages, the first one contains far more text, and there's a substantial difference in the effort and time needed to create each document. Without establishing a standard for what constitutes one unit of measure, estimates can vary greatly for products of the same type, and the unit of measure loses its value.

Once you have identified the appropriate unit of measure for each product, begin the process of estimating the product size. One of the best resources for this is your organization's own historical data from projects of similar size and scope. What happens if you don't have historical data? It's simple: You guess! Make your best engineering judgment to estimate the size. Don't spend so much time on the estimate that you fall into the "paralysis through analysis" trap. If your team is estimating size for the first time, its estimate will inevitably be off the mark, but you can minimize the margin of error. The most effective way to do so is to break the product down into small pieces, then estimate the size of the small pieces.

For example, if you are writing a book and are struggling to estimate how long it will be, you could instead estimate the length of each chapter based on the chapters you have already written. Of course, some chapters will be longer than expected, while others will be shorter, but the estimation errors will tend to cancel each other out. Let's say you have estimated that two chapters will be 15 pages each, totaling 30 pages together. It's quite possible that one chapter will be 50 percent longer, or 22.5 pages long, while the other chapter will be 50 percent shorter, or 7.5 pages long, but the estimation error of each estimate will cancel each other out, and the two chapters added together will total approximately 30 pages as estimated. Breaking the product down into small pieces is an effective way to take advantage of the error estimation cancellation factor and yields more accurate product size estimates.

It's important for you to track and refine your estimates throughout the life of the project. If you don't have historical data at the beginning of the project, the data captured in the current project will become historical data for your future use. Reassure your team members that estimation will become easier as they gain experience and compile useful data.

If I asked you to guess how many one-inch-diameter marbles would fit into a one-gallon jar, you might spend a lot of time trying to figure it out based on the size of the marbles, the volume of the jar, and the amount of space between the marbles. Now let's say I told you that the one-gallon jar holds 623 marbles, then asked you to estimate how many one-inch diameter marbles would fit into a two-gallon jar. It wouldn't take you long to estimate that the two-gallon jar holds 1,246 marbles. This may not be the exact number of marbles in the jar, but it's probably pretty close. If project team members have just one historical data point, they'll be able to produce more accurate estimates faster.

It's possible to accurately extrapolate the number of marbles in the jar because the unit of measure is consistent for both the marbles and the jar. Also, there's a strong correlation between the volume of the jar and the number of marbles that will fit into it. When you make initial estimates, you may select the wrong unit of measure or data points that don't correlate. Always analyze the historical data, if available, to find the most reliable predictor of size. Once you determine the right units and correlations, your estimates will be much more accurate.

Defining Quality Objectives

Now that you have identified all the work products and estimated their respective sizes, you have almost enough information to estimate the work associated with developing the products. The final pieces of data you need are the quality objectives for each project. Building quality into products can require quality-specific products and processes such as draft documents or reviews, so these products and processes should be identified and included in the PBS.

When determining the quality objectives for a product, remember that not all products are created equal. Let's say that you are designing a new building. Your blueprints must be of excellent quality, but quality is less important for the project's internal meeting minutes. Defective blueprints could harm every part of the project, but misspelled words in meeting minutes would have a relatively minor project impact. This is an extreme example, but our point is that you cannot give equal weight to all of the products' quality objectives.

Building quality into the product development process reduces rework and costs, helps the team adhere to the schedule, and boosts product quality. When one considers that 45 percent of the work on the average project is rework, it becomes apparent that building quality into the work products is a key to success. Figure 7-5 shows additional columns that can be added to the PBS template to identify the quality objectives, including quality control and quality assurance, for each product. Examples of *quality control* techniques are discussed in more detail in Chapter 13. These include walk-throughs, in which the product developer reviews the product in the presence of the project team, and peer reviews, in which team members review the product in detail with regard to its requirements, design, and standards. *Quality assurance* techniques include the use of process audits to verify that a product was built using the approved

FIGURE 7-5: Planning for Quality Control and Quality Assurance

PBS #	Product	Quality Control	Quality Assurance
1.0	**Management products**		
1.1	PBS	None	No
1.2	WBS	Peer review	No
1.3	Master schedule	Walk-through	No
1.4	Status reports	None	No
2.0	**Technical products**		
2.1	Storyboard	Peer review	Sample <=50%
2.2	Draft	Peer review	Yes
2.2.1	Draft of Chapter 1	Peer review	Yes
2.2.2	Draft of Chapter 2	Peer review	Yes

process. Sometimes, poor product quality is so damaging that a team will give up near the end of the project, refusing to spend any more time or money to improve quality. This is a very unfortunate situation that better planning and execution of the project can prevent.

By determining all products' quality requirements during the PBS development process, you are forced to analyze each product's importance relative to the overall project, and you can account for the work that will be performed to ensure quality and build more accurate project schedules and cost estimates.

In Brief

When creating the PBS for your project, remember that *all* of the products to be developed must be defined so that the plan can successfully guide the work. Leaving products out means that the project will begin over budget and behind schedule. In addition to identifying each product, you must estimate its size. When possible, it's best to use historical data to estimate rather than engineering judgment. Finally, you will define the quality objectives for each product. Together, these steps will help you build a project plan that accurately accounts for all products, their specifications, and the effort that will go into ensuring their quality.

Suggested Reading and Resources

ABT Corporation. "Core Competencies for Project Managers," *Trends in Software Management,* **April 24, 2000.** The authors assert that PMs should divide their core competencies into soft and hard skills. The soft skills are based on years of feedback from customers and include leadership, flexibility, sound business judgment, trustworthiness, effective communication, coaching and mentoring, active listening, setting and managing expectations, negotiating, and conflict resolution. Hard skills include project initiation, planning, estimating, and controlling.

Bennis, Warren, and Patricia Ward Biederman. *Genius: The Secrets of Creative Collaboration.* **Reading, MA: Perseus Books, 1997.** This is a book about great teams. The take-home lessons at the end of the book are apt descriptions of the most successful teams, like the Skunk Works team—a term that has become synonymous with secret, groundbreaking technological work—and the Manhattan Project team. That none of us are as smart as all of us is a valuable lesson reiterated throughout the book.

Cole, Peter S. *How to Write a Statement of Work,* **5th ed. Vienna, VA: Management Concepts, 2003.** The SOW describes the products and services the project is expected to deliver. Because the WBS is based on planned project work and deliverables, the WBS is often used as an outline for the SOW. In his book, Cole provides practical, detailed guidance, including discussions on how to choose the right type of SOW, performance-based service contracting, and the use of a statement of objectives (SOO). He provides a model SOW format and identifies common problem areas and discusses how to address them. An appendix describes how to analyze an SOW critically.

Hooks, Ivy F., and Kristin A. Farry. *Customer-Centered Products: Creating Successful Products through Smart Requirements Management.* **New York: AMACOM, 2001.** This book is an excellent guide for PMs, offering advice and insight based on years of experience. The authors emphasize the importance of PMs allocating resources, defining and enforcing processes, educating personnel, and measuring the impact of processes on final product quality.

Note

1. For a comprehensive and helpful discussion of the SOW, see Peter S. Cole, *How to Write a Statement of Work,* 5th ed. (Vienna, VA: Management Concepts, 2003).

8 Identifying the Work

In Chapter 7, we discussed the process a team uses to identify all of the products that will be created during the execution of the project. We list these products in the product breakdown structure (PBS). As shown in Figure 8-1, the next step in the process is to identify how these products will be created. This involves the development of the work breakdown structure (WBS), which documents project activities and their respective effort.

While the PBS identifies the items to be produced and the WBS identifies the work to be done, the documents are created using similar processes, and both are critical to the development of the plan.

FIGURE 8-1: Defining the Work

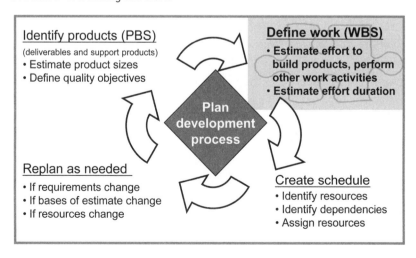

Identify products (PBS)
(deliverables and support products)
• Estimate product sizes
• Define quality objectives

Define work (WBS)
• Estimate effort to build products, perform other work activities
• Estimate effort duration

Plan development process

Replan as needed
• If requirements change
• If bases of estimate change
• If resources change

Create schedule
• Identify resources
• Identify dependencies
• Assign resources

Figure 8-2 illustrates the general process for developing the WBS. Obviously, there is work associated with creating each product, so it's only natural that the PBS is the key input for the creation of the WBS. In turn, the WBS is used to create the project schedule, which we discuss in Chapter 9. The project schedule tells us when the project will be complete and how much it will cost.

FIGURE 8-2: Identifying the Work Effort Needed to Complete Your Project

Account for *all* effort to be expended!

Identify direct product effort	→	Identify other effort	→	Estimate work duration

- Determine how much effort will be needed to build PBS items
- Contract-specified work activities
- Meetings
- Technical leadership
- Review historical data
- Divide work into small activities
- Record basis of estimate

The Purpose of the WBS

The purpose of the WBS is straightforward: to identify all of the work that must be done to successfully complete the project. Failing to identify all of the work has the same effect as leaving products out of the PBS—it puts the project behind schedule and over budget from the start. Work that isn't accounted for in the WBS will not be planned or budgeted for in the schedule, but it still has to be done to complete the project. The PM will then have to adjust the schedule and resource plan to accommodate the forgotten work. Not only does additional work cost more money and take more time, but it also diminishes the confidence of the project's stakeholders in your team. To help avoid having to report to your stakeholders that your project is behind schedule and over budget, make sure your WBS is comprehensive.

The WBS also plays a valuable role in identifying the skill sets and re-sources required to complete the project. We return to an example from Chapter 7. Let's say your project team is building a city park. The team will quickly determine that the project needs a park designer to develop the plans, tradespeople to install playground equipment, carpenters to build shelters and park benches, and plumbers to install water fountains. These skill sets are relatively easy to identify because they relate directly to the creation or installation of the identified products, but identifying supporting labor is not always so simple. For example, parks must meet certain safety requirements to pass code inspections. An additional proj-ect resource, such as a safety compliance officer, may be needed to help the team fulfill these requirements.

Your team's goal should be to incorporate *all* known requirements in the project plan.[1] Do not wait until something goes wrong—until the park fails a safety inspection, for example. If this happens, your project team might have to spend money and time removing or rebuilding equipment. Avoid problems like these by being proactive while the team is drafting the WBS.

Preparing to Build the WBS

The WBS is typically easier to prepare than is the PBS, mostly because the work done to prepare for the PBS can be reused for the WBS process. The WBS process is largely the same for projects of all sizes, and it can be completed in the same amount of time as a PBS—less than a day for a small project and a couple of days for a large one.

First, review the preparation activities for the PBS. Did the team have everything it needed to go through the process efficiently and effectively? If so, collect the same project artifacts (documents) the team used to create the PBS, including the PBS itself. Ask the same team members to participate and reserve an appropriate meeting space. If the PBS process did not go smoothly because the team lacked necessary resources, figure out what lessons the team learned and correct any problems before work-ing on the WBS.

Next, collect project information. The PBS, the SOW, and the contract are the most critical documents for the WBS creation process. These documents identify many of the project activities that the team must execute, so they must be referenced during the WBS process. If they are not, you might fail to document key activities. If your team doesn't perform a key contract activity, your company could be held in breach of contract.

The PM should also identify any internal activities that must be executed. These might include internal status meetings, line management reviews, and corporate quality audits. What would happen if you did not plan for the status meetings? Let's say that your project is scheduled to last one year. The team is required to conduct an hour-long weekly status meeting. Each status meeting takes 16 hours of staff time (16 team members multiplied by one hour of time), equivalent to two person-days of time. Over one year (52 weeks), status meetings consume 104 person-days. Just imagine how not accounting for 104 person-days of time will affect your project's schedule!

Now, how will neglecting to plan for status meetings affect your budget? Let's say your team has 16 members, and the average hourly cost of each team member is $25. Each status meeting then costs the project $400. If the team will attend 52 meetings in one year, you'll have a budgetary shortfall of $20,800! Omitting the status meetings means you'll begin the project over budget.

You can gather additional useful data for the WBS by reviewing previous projects completed by the organization and analyzing those that most closely resemble the size and scope of the current project. Returning to our park project example, most cities have a number of parks and some kind of time-tracking system. The project team should review the time-tracking system to determine how much time was spent building similar parks. This analysis should cover all work for the previous projects, including support activities like reviews and status meetings. The team can then use this data to estimate how long it will take to execute the current project. Analyzing other projects will help reduce the risk of missing key activities and will strengthen your ability to provide a solid basis of estimate.

The next step in preparing to build the WBS is choosing the WBS team. If the PBS team performed well and included representatives from all project groups, then putting together the WBS team is easy—just use the same team. But if the PBS team was deficient in some way, select different people if possible for the WBS team, making sure to identify all of the sub-groups contributing to the project and choosing at least one representative from each group.

Finally, because the WBS development process is so similar to the PBS process, you will need to gather the same supplies you used to create the PBS, including Post-it® notes, markers, computers, and perhaps a projector. You also must reserve a meeting space. Make sure the meeting room is large enough to comfortably hold the WBS development team and will facilitate uninterrupted work.

Developing the WBS and Defining the Work

Conducting the WBS creation meeting will be very similar to conducting the PBS creation meeting. The goal of this process is to estimate the effort required for, and the duration of, each project activity based on the work identified in the PBS. Figure 8-3 shows a partial sample WBS.

FIGURE 8-3: Identifying Each Work Activity

WBS #	Work Activity	Work Type	Est. Hrs.	BOE	Actual Hrs.
1.0	**Compose Book**		2332.0	calculation	
1.1	**Plan Project**	None	11.5	calculation	
1.1.1	Create WBS	Level of effort	5.0	from PBS	
1.1.2	Create master schedule	Level of effort	6.0	from PBS	
1.1.3	Deliver master schedule	Milestone	0.5	pages	
1.2	**Create Book**		2297.	calculation	
1.2.1	Create Storyboard	Level of effort	170.0	from PBS	
1.2.2	Create Draft	Level of effort	1344.0	calculation	
1.2.2.1	Draft Chapter 1	Level of effort	84.0	from PBS	
1.2.2.2	Draft Chapter 2	Level of effort	84.0	from PBS	

Start the meeting by reviewing the PBS and identifying the activities required to produce those products. As the team identifies the work to construct each product, the meeting facilitator should write each work activity's name on a Post-it® note, one work activity per note.

You will structure the WBS just as you structured the PBS. Divide the work activities into two groups, management and technical (Figure 8-4).

- *Management work* is associated with running the project.
- *Technical work* is associated with engineering the products.

Then decompose each group into sub-groups of external and internal activities:

- *External management work* is associated with running the project and is delivered to the customer (for example, communicating the schedule status).
- *Internal management work* is associated with running the project but is not visible to the customer (for example, monitoring profit).
- *External technical work* is associated with engineering the products that are delivered to the customer (for example, designing blueprints)
- *Internal technical work* is associated with engineering products but is not visible to the customer (for example, creating design templates).

Create a category under each of the four sub-groups of work (external management, internal management, external technical, and internal technical) for each project area, such as design, engineering, and testing. Use a Post-it® note or sheet of paper stuck to the wall to designate these categories. Your WBS team should then collaborate to determine which activities fall under each category. Adhere each note bearing a work activity to the wall under the appropriate heading.

As you identify the work associated with creating each product, remember that most products will require more than one associated activ-

FIGURE 8-4: Brainstorming Work

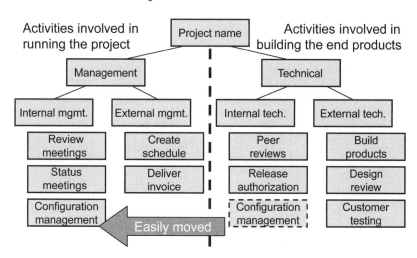

ity. For example, if you must develop a set of blueprints, decompose the development of the blueprints into individual activities such as developing a draft of the blueprints, conducting a safety review, modifying the blueprints based on the safety review, reviewing plans with the customer, modifying the blueprints based on customer feedback, getting final customer sign-off, and finalizing the blueprints. As you can see, the creation of one product deliverable can launch many discrete supporting activities that each require effort to complete.

After the team has identified all of the work associated with creating the products, examine the SOW and the contract to identify work that the team is contractually obligated to perform but that does not lead to the creation of a product. This work may include customer reviews and status meetings. Also, identify internal work activities that may not always be directly linked to a product, such as technical leadership for software projects, project management, and foreman oversight. You must include all of this work in the WBS. It is critical to the success of the project, even if it does not have a direct link to developing final products.

When you are confident that all of the work activities have been identified, document the WBS. Spreadsheets work very well for this. Note each work activity's name, assign a unique number to each one, and include additional data about each activity, including the PBS number of the associated product and the team's estimate of how long the activity will take.

Estimating Effort

Estimating the size of a job can help you determine how long the job will take to complete. That's why we document the sizes of all products in the PBS before we create the WBS.

When estimating the effort needed to perform a work activity, it's important to understand that you are creating an estimate for the time team members will spend doing the activity; you are not estimating calendar time. For each activity, you'll estimate the number of hours required for one individual to complete the task. You'll estimate the amount of calendar time activities will take when you create the project schedule.

Proper definition of work activities, along with data from past projects of similar size and scope, can help you estimate the time required to complete them. But historical data by itself is not enough. Couple it with the product size estimates from the current PBS when making work activity estimates. Remember that your ability to develop estimates will improve each time you go through the estimating process, especially as team members track their estimates and compare them with actual data. Note that the improvement does not come automatically. Rather, it comes as a result of a deliberate continuous improvement effort: document your estimates; compare estimates with actual figures; and work proactively to improve the process.

If your organization has records from previous projects that show the hours charged for each work activity, you can compare the size of the past products to that of the current products. Returning once again to the city park example, let's say that your team plans to install 20 wooden benches on the park grounds. The historical data tells you that one city park has 10 benches, which took 50 hours to install, and another park has 15 benches, which took 62 hours to install. So what is the historic average installation rate per park bench? Add the hours spent on installation (50 hours + 62 hours) and divide the total (112 hours) by the total number of benches (10 + 15 = 25). Each bench took an average of 4.5 hours to install. Multiply this rate by the number of benches in your current project (20). It should take about 90 hours to install the benches in the new park.

Of course, estimation is not always this easy, and you won't have historical data for every work activity on your project. When you don't have relevant historical data, you'll guess how long activities will take. As a rule, make sure that no task is more 80 hours in duration. It is easier to estimate the duration of work if it's broken into smaller chunks. If we didn't have historical data on the park bench installations, for example, we wouldn't estimate how long it would take to install all of them, but rather how long it would take to install one. This estimate could then be extrapolated to the remaining benches.

It is also easier to track work activities when they are broken down into short-duration tasks. Let's say that the PM for the park project tells a tradesperson that he or she has 90 hours to install 20 park benches, waits until the 90 hours have passed to check on the tradesperson's progress, then learns that he or she has installed just 15 benches. The project is now behind schedule and over budget. But by breaking the activity down, the PM can track progress and take corrective action much sooner. What if the PM had checked in after 16 hours? Based on the estimate of 4.5 hours installation time per bench, he or she would have expected to find three benches installed and a fourth partially done. When the PM found that only two were complete, he or she would have realized that the installation was behind schedule. After only 16 hours, the PM could have worked to resolve the delay. This is why it is important for the project team to track and refine its estimates throughout the life of the project.

In Brief

The purpose of the WBS is simple: to document and quantify all of the work that must be accomplished to successfully complete the project. Failing to document some work activities puts the project behind schedule and over budget from the beginning because these activities will not be planned or budgeted for. After your team has determined and documented all of the activities for the project, including those that don't lead to the creation of a product, you will estimate the amount of time needed to perform each activity. The project schedule, which you'll create next, will be based on the WBS.

Suggested Reading and Resources

Demarco, Tom, and Timothy Lister. *Peopleware: Productive Projects and Teams,* 2nd ed. New York: Dorset House Publishing Company, 1999. This classic book presents the human dimension of technical development projects. The authors, who collected data from development projects for over 20 years, have more than 500 project histories in their database. They posit that the high number of project failures is not due to technological failures; rather, human issues like project management, communications, high turnover, and lack of motivation are to blame. Given these trends, managers must create a culture that allows people to work effectively.

Haugan, Gregory T. *Work Breakdown Structures of Projects, Programs, and Enterprises.* Vienna, VA: Management Concepts, 2008. In this book, Haugan draws on the definition of a project provided in the *Guide to the Project Management Body of Knowledge (PMBOK® Guide)* to recommend an approach to developing a WBS. He provides a process to develop the WBS and a checklist for the project team to use to evaluate the adequacy of the WBS. Chapter 5 describes in detail the many uses of a WBS, and Chapter 10 provides several WBS examples and descriptions of them.

Humphrey, Watts S. *Managing Technical People: Innovation, Teamwork, and the Software Process.* **Reading, MA: Addison-Wesley, 1997.** Humphrey, drawing from 50 years of experience to write this book, believes that history is a marvelous teacher as long as we are willing to learn. The key is to understand and respect people and to follow sound management principles, applying them with a healthy sprinkling of common sense. This book adds several chapters to Humphrey's earlier book, *Managing for Innovation: Leading Technical People,* including one that describes the power of a process improvement strategy. Other topics include respecting individuals and motivating technical and professional people; professional discipline; developing technical talent; managing innovation teams; and managing change.

Humphrey, Watts S. *Introduction to the Personal Software Process.* **Reading, MA: Addison-Wesley, 1997.** This excellent book describes the personal software process (PSP) and offers an approach to implementing it. PSP is a methodology based on process improvement principles that enable developers to consistently and efficiently develop high-quality products. PSP teaches developers to measure and manage the quality of their work using defect density, defect removal rates, and yield-productivity ratios to analyze size, time-in phase, defect, and schedule measures.

McConnell, Steve. *Software Estimation: Demystifying the Black Art.* **Redmond, WA: Microsoft Press, 2006.** Identifying the work that a project will require is one of the major challenges in project planning and among the key reasons why projects fail. In this book, McConnell demystifies the "black art" of software estimation by providing a proven set of procedures, easy-to-understand formulas, and guidelines for developing realistic schedule, effort, and cost estimates. Readers can apply McConnell's estimation approaches to small, large, traditional, or agile projects—a software development methodology that breaks a project into small pieces called "sprints."

Note

1. Project managers and developers must take into account that not all requirements are known at the beginning of a development effort. Some requirements are likely to be discovered during the development process, and new requirements will inevitably surface. One reason this happens is because we learn more about what the customer needs as we perform development activities. This is why your development process must be able to accommodate a degree of requirements change throughout the course of the project.

9 Establishing a Schedule

In this chapter, we explain how to develop a resource-loaded schedule, which will answer two very important questions: "When will the project be done?" and "How much will the project cost?" Figure 9-1 illustrates how the creation of the schedule fits into the plan development process (PDP).

The project schedule is also used to set and communicate stakeholders' expectations, solidify the project team's and external stakeholders' commitment to the milestones for which each group is responsible, and gain the project sponsor's commitment to provide resources, including person-

FIGURE 9-1: Creating the Schedule

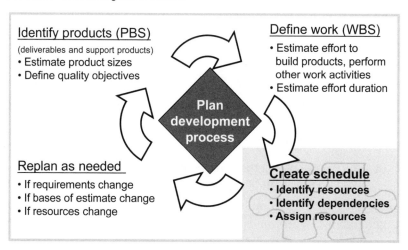

nel, budgets, equipment, and time. In short, the schedule is used for more than just tracking status and is critical to the success of the project.

For the project schedule to be effective, it must be maintained throughout the life of the project. Changes in the project dependencies (for example, the environment, requirements, tasks, or resources) must be noted in the schedule so that it continues to guide the project work and manage stakeholder expectations.

The Purpose of the Schedule

A well-crafted schedule can answer a number of questions about the project's status and health. It can tell us when the project will be complete, how much it will cost, what resources are needed, when the next milestone will be met, and if the project is ahead of or behind schedule. It can also be used to answer "what if" questions, such as "What happens to the project if a team member is removed?", "What happens if a new person joins the team?", or "What happens if a new project task, milestone, or requirement is added to the schedule?"

The schedule can be used to analyze resource allocation and cost. Let's say that for the city park project we've been discussing, two surveyors, one who will cost the project $15 per hour and another who will cost the project $20 per hour, will survey the site. You've estimated that it will take them 40 hours, or two and a half days, to complete the survey. The cost of the survey will then be $700 ([20 hours * $15] + [20 hours * $20]). But let's assume that the surveyors are available to the park project for only four hours a day. You will then allocate them to the surveying task at a rate of 50 percent and will estimate that the task will take five days. (It will, however, still cost $700, because it will take the same number of hours as originally estimated.)

In addition to helping the team determine the cost and duration of project tasks, the schedule is used to track the project's performance. Monitoring the completion status of each task is critical. It is best to break long-duration activities into short-duration tasks known as inch stones so that progress (or lack thereof) can be quickly ascertained. This approach enables prompt replanning if progress is not being made. Remember that each project task should last less than 80 hours. If the construction of a playground for the city park is scheduled to last three months, we might break it into several one- or two-week tasks, such as installing and testing the swing set, merry-go-round, and monkey bars. We will then track the status of each of these tasks. If the installation of the swing set takes six days, not the scheduled five, we will know immediately that we have to make up a day of schedule time. We can correct the problem quickly, perhaps by adding workers to the project so that the merry-go-round and monkey bars can be installed simultaneously.

What would happen if every one-week task took just one extra day? After 12 weeks, the project would be 12 days, or 20 percent, behind schedule. Attempting to fix a one-day schedule delay at the start of a three-month task is much easier than attempting to fix a 12-day slip at the end of a three-month task. That's why it's preferable to track work using inch stones, not long-duration milestones.

Transitioning from the WBS

Transitioning from the work breakdown structure (WBS) to a schedule must be done carefully, or it can lead to the development of an unrealistic project schedule, which will lead to unrealistic stakeholder expectations (Figure 9-2). The first step to building a realistic schedule is to set the parameters of your scheduling software so that non-workdays (weekends, holidays, and vacations) don't show up in the schedule as workdays. If your team's normal workweek is Monday through Friday, verify that your scheduling tool[1] is set up to use Monday through Friday as its workdays. Most tools don't automatically exclude holidays as workdays, so you'll have to exclude them manually.

Then, enter information on the project team members into the resource section of the scheduling tool, including each team member's hourly rate so that you can calculate project labor costs and establish an accurate budget for each task. Most scheduling tools allow you to set up calen-

FIGURE 9-2: Transitioning from the WBS

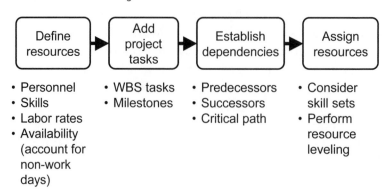

dars and availability for each person on the project. Let's say that one of your equipment installers will work 20 hours a week on your project. You would set his or her availability to 50 percent in the scheduling tool. When you assign the equipment installer to a 20-hour project task, the scheduling software should automatically set the duration of the task to 40 hours because the installer is available only 50 percent of the time.

If you know team members' vacation schedules, you can mark days out of the office as non-working days, and the tool will automatically factor in those constraints when it creates the schedule. If you don't know when team members plan to be out, make an educated guess about how much each person will be available. Let's assume each person gets two weeks of vacation and one week of sick leave and that your organization observes ten holidays a year. That means that each team member is available for 1880 hours a year (40 hours per week * 47 weeks per year) maximum—not 2080 hours (40 hours per week * 52 weeks per year). Neglecting to factor in vacation and sick time can cause a project to fall behind schedule.

Next, you will add the project tasks to the schedule. All of the activities in the WBS should go into the project schedule. Usually, the work activities listed in the WBS support the creation of products documented in the product breakdown structure (PBS). Items listed in the PBS make natural schedule milestones. Let's say that you're developing a design document.

The related work activities might include performing analysis, drafting the design document, reviewing the design document, and updating the design document. These lead to a complete design document, which can be considered a milestone.

Then you should review the WBS to identify dependencies between work tasks. Here you will determine predecessor/successor relationships between tasks that are dependent on each other. Think back to the city park project discussed earlier. The park site must be surveyed before it can be excavated and excavated before the foundation can be poured. The survey is a predecessor task to the excavation; the pouring of the foundation is a successor task to the excavation. If the survey is delayed, there will be a corresponding delay in the excavation. Establishing predecessor/successor relationships can help you manage the schedule. You can alter the project's completion date if, for example, a work activity is delayed because preceding tasks have not been completed.

Teams often neglect to identify tasks that must be accomplished by the customer. For example, we worked on a software development project to replace an outdated system. The customer was responsible for converting the legacy data from the old system. We were dependent on the customer's completing the data conversion task before we could begin acceptance testing and production, so it was critical to our project's success to identify the date by which we needed the customer to have finished the conversion. We didn't just show up on the due date to ask for the data—we reviewed the status of the conversion task at each weekly meeting. Our monitoring the task encouraged the customer to better allocate resources to get it done and gave our team opportunities to identify and resolve data conversion issues the customer experienced. If the customer is behind schedule, you can use the schedule to demonstrate how the delay will affect the project.

After all of the project tasks have been added to the schedule, it is time to assign team members to tasks. Some pointers that may seem obvious but are very important include:

- Make sure each individual has the skills and experience required to accomplish the assigned task.

- Monitor each team member's allocation level. Someone who is dedicated to your project full time should not be allocated to more than or less than 40 hours of assigned work in a week.

- Although the work week typically includes a certain number of hours, all these hours are not necessarily designated productive hours. For example, individuals may be required to attend non-project related briefings or information-sharing sessions.

Resource leveling is the act of evening out the tasks that project team members are assigned so that each person has approximately the same workload. Unfortunately, there's no easy way to do this, so this process is usually one of the more tedious and time-consuming aspects of building a resource-loaded schedule. This is another area to document and improve upon over time, so that future project planning is based on actual experience.

Reviewing the Schedule

A project schedule can consist of hundreds or even thousands of tasks, depending on the size of the project, so a thorough review before sharing the schedule with outside stakeholders is essential. Reviewers should have diverse skill sets and should include key members of the project team, other PMs with experience leading projects of similar size and scope, key members of your management team, and the project control officer (if you use earned-value management). Reviewers should answer the following questions about the schedule:

- Is the schedule reasonable?

- Do I have all of the resources needed to complete the project?

- Does the schedule meet all of the project's requirements (such as due dates or budget constraints)?

- Have all predecessor/successor relationships between tasks been documented?

- Were the project's resources leveled appropriately?

- Was non-working time set in the schedule?

- Do all team members have the skills and equipment needed to complete their assigned tasks?

The team will then update the schedule as necessary based on feedback from the schedule review. If the modifications are significant, a second review should be scheduled to make sure all of the changes were incorporated into the schedule and to ensure the revised schedule makes sense.

Once the schedule has been reviewed and approved by the reviewers, it should be submitted to your line management for approval. PMs are typically dependent on line management to provide planned resources (personnel, budgets, equipment, and time) on time; management's sign-off indicates a commitment to give you the resources needed to execute the plan. Be advised, however, that you are likely to have to coordinate closely with your management to encourage them to keep their commitments.

Communicating with Stakeholders

A complete, reviewed, signed, and well-maintained project schedule is a valuable tool that should be used to communicate with all project stakeholders and justify your team's needs. Primary uses of the project schedule include facilitating communication with and between project team members and encouraging their commitment to the project's mission. The schedule:

- Tells team members when work is due and how many hours they are expected to put into it

- Helps team members determine how their assigned tasks relate to other team members' tasks

- Facilitates teamwork; when problems arise, connected team members can work together to streamline future tasks

- Illustrates the "big picture" of the project.

The team should review the schedule regularly to make sure the team is on track and working on the scheduled assignments.

The project schedule is also used to set stakeholder expectations. Stakeholders often question the duration or cost of project tasks. A detailed project schedule that lays out every work activity will enable you to have a fact-based conversation with your stakeholders. If a stakeholder wants to cut your project's schedule or funding, you can ask him or her to review the documented project tasks and identify the tasks that do not need to be done. He or she will likely be hard-pressed to identify any tasks that aren't necessary and will not be able to justify reducing the allotted time or funding. If you do not have a PBS, WBS, or schedule, you might be forced to accept less funding or a rushed timeline because you do not have accurate estimates of the resources and time you will need.

You can use the project schedule to run "what if" scenarios. Sometimes a manager who is not associated with your project will ask to pull one of your team members for other work. Remove the team member from your schedule and show the manager how the loss would affect your project. Losing a team member usually delays a project, so this may be enough to dissuade the manager. But what if management deems it appropriate to pull the person anyway? You can then use the revised project schedule to guide the remaining work—and as a tool for explaining to stakeholders why the schedule has slipped.

It is important for project team members to understand the value of the schedule and how it is to be used so that they take the time and care necessary to develop a quality schedule. This may be a new experience for your team. Most people working on projects have not used PBSs and WBSs to create schedules. But schedules developed without this detailed information are not useful and usually fall by the wayside. If you build your schedule the right way, maintain it regularly, and communicate any changes to all stakeholders, your project team will realize its value.

In Brief

The project schedule tells us when the project is going to be done and how much it will cost. It also is a tool for communicating with stakeholders, including your team members, and setting their expectations, so it must be a living document, constantly updated to reflect changes in project dependencies or team composition. The schedule should be based on the work activities you have documented in the WBS. You must determine which activities are dependent on one another and what tasks the customer must complete, and carefully review the schedule before sharing it with stakeholders.

Suggested Reading and Resources

McConnell, Steve. *Rapid Development*. Redmond, Washington: Microsoft Press, 1996. McConnell posits that rapid development is not a "glitzy methodology"; rather, it simply makes use of good practices, time, and effort to achieve an effective development process. He advocates choosing effective practices that orient specifically toward achieving schedule objectives. McConnell discusses major topics in development, including partnering, as well as 43 specific best practices.

Paulk, Mark C., Charles V. Weber, Suzanne M. Garcia, Mary Beth Chrissis, and Marilyn W. Bush. *Key Practices of the Capability Maturity Model,* Version 1.1. Pittsburgh, PA: Software Engineering Institute, Carnegie-Mellon University, 1993. Available online at www.sei.cmu .edu/publications/documents/93.reports/93.tr.025.html. The *Capability Maturity Model (CMM) for Software,* Version 1.1, is a relatively short document—only 64 pages. The *Key Practices of the CMM,* Version 1.1, is much more extensive and describes the practices for each of the 18 key process areas. Both documents are organized by a set of common features: the commitment and ability to perform; activities performed; measurement and analysis; and implementation verification. Applying these practices to projects and organizations is very helpful in improving the development process.

Wiegers, Karl E. "Stop Promising Miracles." *Software Development Magazine* **(February 2000). Available online at www.ddj.com/dept/architect/184414570.** It is common in project management to unrealistically over-promise deliverables. Whether due to optimism, management pressure, artificial milestones, or time-to-market concerns, PMs can control this problem by improving deliverable estimations—the subject of Wiegers' article. Wiegers encourages PMs to develop experienced-based estimates, incorporate contingency buffers, consider project risks, build quality-assurance into the process and the products, and use proven methods to develop estimates.

Wiegers, Karl E. "Habits of Effective Analysts," *Software Development Magazine,* **vol. 8, no. 10 (October 2000): 62–65. Available online at www.processimpact.com/articles/analyst_habits.html.** In this article, Wiegers provides thoughtful and provocative insights about the role of the requirements engineer (also called the requirements analyst, business analyst, systems analyst, or requirements manager). He emphasizes that requirements engineering has its own skill set and body of knowledge, which are given scant attention in most computer science educational curricula and even by most systems and software engineering organizations. A competent requirements engineer must combine communication, facilitation, and interpersonal skills with technical and business knowledge to elicit and analyze requirements. Wiegers recommends that every organization develop an experienced cadre of requirements analysts, even if requirements engineering is not considered a vital function for every project.

Note

1. Be sure to consult with your colleagues to learn about available automated tools prior to selecting them for your project. In our experience, the complexity of some available tools renders them difficult to use on a project.

III

Project Execution
How to Minimize the Risk of Future Failure

10 Executing the Plan

So you've developed a plan. Now what? It's time to execute the plan. We've identified four key techniques you can use to ensure the success of your project: creating mini-schedules, documenting and following team processes, replanning often, and keeping the right team.

Mini-schedules are based on inch stones, short-duration tasks that help you monitor progress and replan quickly if the project heads off track. Because projects can span long periods of time, it's important to make sure the team stays focused on the work by using near-term goals. The best way to do this is to develop mini-schedules, detailed subsets of the overall project schedule. These mini-schedules give the project team clarity of purpose and the incentive to work toward short-term goals that position the team to meet its long-term objectives.

The second technique, documenting and following team processes, fosters repeatability, consistency, and continuous improvement. If members of your team use different processes to complete the same work, your project will not be predictable, and you'll likely end up with work of inconsistent quality. Without documented processes, the skill level of the individual doing the work determines its quality. By documenting team processes and making sure those processes are followed, you enable all team members to perform the work consistently, which leads to consistent output. Consistent output improves your ability to estimate. Finally, as the team becomes more familiar with the processes, it can improve the processes, which will lead to greater product quality and personal and project efficiency and effectiveness.

The third technique, frequent replanning, helps you keep the plan current. You cannot create the perfect plan, no matter how hard you try; circumstances or events that you didn't anticipate will always arise. When the unforeseen happens, you must adjust the plan. This is the only way the plan will to continue to guide the work. If the plan is not maintained, it is no longer useful to the project team or the stakeholders. In our experience, a major failure of most projects is neglecting the project plan.

Finally, keeping the right team is critical to the success of the project. One of your responsibilities as a PM is to encourage your team to follow the plan and its processes until doing so becomes second nature. If you are constantly changing the composition of the team, it will never have the chance to mature.

Creating Mini-Schedules

Inch stones are much easier to stay focused on than milestones and are good motivating tools. A mini-schedule is composed of several inch stones. The weight-loss story of Tina Adkins, Steve Brady's sister-in-law, illustrates the motivating power of setting mini-schedules. Tina, who originally weighed 275 pounds, lost 135 pounds through exercise and diet. Tina's plan called for her to lose 100 pounds in one year. To accomplish her goal, she planned to work out 208 times and eat 1,200 healthy meals in that year.

Imagine how daunting this plan must have seemed at the beginning of the year! Tina hadn't eaten right or exercised in a long time. If she had focused only on her long-term goal, she likely would have become discouraged quickly. So she broke her plan into smaller, more attainable inch stones. She planned daily menus, developed weekly workout plans, and established weekly weight-loss targets. These inch stones—three healthy meals a day, four workouts a week, and two pounds lost per week—made it easier for Tina to reach her long-term goal because she was able to succeed, week after week, at meeting the short-term objectives.

Mini-schedules for a project work the same way. They set short-term objectives for the team. They also provide a framework for regular status reviews. By tracking the project using mini-schedules, you can confirm that the team is making progress toward the overall project objectives. Deviance from a mini-schedule is an indicator of potential problems. Catching and fixing issues early is the key to keeping the project on track.

We used mini-schedules when developing a new software program that was expected to comprise 100,000 lines of code and take about nine months to complete. We broke the project into five "builds," or phases, each with its own mini-schedule. The project team's technical lead created a mini-schedule for the first build. (Mini-schedules tend to be more effective when established and administered by team leads.) He identified the screens and functionality that would be created during the build and distributed coding assignments to the developers on the team.

Each developer focused on completing four or five screens and 2,000 to 3,000 lines of code for the first build—not on the 120 screens and 100,000 lines of code the final project would comprise. The technical lead met regularly with the developers, monitored their progress, and helped resolve issues to keep the project moving forward.

Meanwhile, the PM scheduled weekly mini-schedule review meetings with the technical lead to track the developers' progress and to make sure the overall project objectives were being accomplished. The technical lead was able to use the mini-schedule to give the PM quantitative reports[1] on the project's status. The PM learned about problems that could have delayed the project as they came up—not months later, when correcting them would have been much more difficult.

Mini-schedules also help a team analyze its own performance. We used the mini-schedule at the end of the first build to quantify our team's performance and take a detailed look at our development processes. We tracked the number of screens developed, the lines of code produced, the density of defects, and variance from the schedule. We then analyzed the team's processes, looking for ways to improve their quality and efficiency, and we implemented actions to improve our processes. This improved the code produced in the subsequent builds.

Finally, the mini-schedule gave the team a mechanism to more effectively communicate the project's status and needs to the stakeholders. We were able to engage the stakeholders early by sharing information about the first build with them. (Stakeholders may lose interest if interaction is limited. See Figure 1-3, which depicts how to keep stakeholders involved throughout the project.) We demonstrated the completed work and allowed them to perform a preliminary test of the system. This hands-on exposure to the software was important in retaining their support throughout the project.

Documenting Processes

When processes aren't documented and followed, project teams end up trying to reinvent the wheel. If you leave decisions on how to do project work up to project team members, you'll end up with work of inconsistent quality. The quality of a product will depend solely on the skill of the individual producing it. But creating and documenting processes yields a repeatable set of steps that foster greater consistency. Using repeatable processes also provides a baseline for performing work, which can be measured and analyzed against the baseline and then improved. In addition, well-documented processes offer a team some protection against staff turnover. New team members can be trained using the team's processes, making it much easier to bring a new person with the right skill set up to speed more quickly.

One of the first steps in documenting team processes is identifying potential processes. Processes can be developed to do project work that is repeatable. Let's examine the process of writing this book. Because this book has several authors, it was important to develop and follow a process so that the chapters would be consistent with one another. We used the same process for writing each of the chapters, whether we were working on Chapter 1 or Chapter 14. First, we created a storyboard that outlined the content for each chapter and developed a template in Microsoft Word that allocated pages for each chapter. The template listed all of the book's chapters and subsections and contained an outline of the key points we planned to discuss in each chapter and subsection. We set the template up to meet the publisher's guidelines for font styles, line spacing, and page margins. The author of each chapter used the template to write his assigned chapter, then submitted the finished chapter to the team for review. Following our internal reviews and after incorporating everyone's feedback, we provided the updated work product to other knowledgeable experts for additional peer reviews. This process reduced errors and resulted in suggestions to help clarify the material and make it even more informative. After the chapters were reviewed and modified, they were incorporated into a single document for delivery to the publisher.

Checklists enhance consistency and can be used to catch many common mistakes. They help prevent problems that could surface later in the project. For a software development project, we developed a code review checklist. One of the checklist questions was "Is the code adequately commented to clearly explain its intended purpose?" If the answer was no, then comments detailing the code were added before the code unit was integrated with the rest of the application. This helped streamline future code modifications, either to correct defects or to enhance system functionality. By improving the code comments before integrating them into the system, we made it more efficient for another team member to update the code during the maintenance and testing phases of the project. Remember, correcting a defect late in a project's life cycle is much more expensive than correcting it earlier.[2]

Improving quality is something that we hear a lot about, but often little or no tangible evidence is available to know if you've truly improved quality. If you document your processes, measure performance, and categorize defects, you can establish quantitative measures of quality.[3]

At the end of the first build for the software development project mentioned earlier, we analyzed the defects we saw in the code and modified our development processes to prevent the same defects from appearing in future builds. We then continued to track the number and types of defects in the code. At the end of the second build, we compared the defect density in the first and second builds. We found that there were fewer defects per thousand lines of code in the second build. Now we had quantitative evidence that our changes had indeed improved the software development process.

Project teams often say they don't define and track their process performance because doing so is too expensive and time-consuming. But this is not necessarily true. As we worked on the software development project, we tracked the time it took to correct one defect. We were thus able to calculate the cost of correcting one defect as well as how much we saved during the second build by changing the processes we had used for the first build. The cost savings were eye-opening for both the project team and line management. Suddenly management was very interested in applying our development techniques and continuous improvement practices on other projects.

Documented processes are also a good training tool for new team members. New people are usually mentored by an existing team member—who is generally pressed for time and does not always do a good job. When teams don't have documented processes, the trainer is likely to forget to talk about parts of the processes because they have become second nature; he or she no longer thinks about them. So the new person is not fully trained and is left to figure out the processes on his or her own.

But if a project team has well-documented processes, a veteran team member can use them to train new team members. This ensures that all of the steps in the processes will be covered during training. The new team member can refer to the documented processes as he or she comes up to speed on the project. This will help him or her become productive more quickly.

Documenting processes may be tedious or time-consuming, but it actually saves time in the long run and results in higher quality products. We recommend incorporating time to document processes into the project plan, thus allocating your team the time and resources needed to do it.

Frequent Replanning

Your plan should guide the work; when the project changes, so should the plan. Changes can stem from the loss of a team member, the addition of new project requirements, a directive from management, delayed delivery of a products, or unforeseen events outside the project, just to name a few causes. Project teams must expect change and develop and implement a process for maintaining the plan so that it can evolve and continue to guide the work.

In the event of a minor change, such as a team member's removal from the project for a month, the corresponding change to the plan might be minor, too—perhaps just an update to the project schedule. But some changes, such as the addition of new requirements, might require a major overhaul of the plan. For example, if the team now has to develop new products, it must repeat the product breakdown structure (PBS) process to define and estimate the new products. Then, after updating the PBS, the team will repeat the work breakdown structure (WBS) process to define how the new products will be developed. Finally, the team will add the new work to the resource-loaded schedule.

As we discussed in Chapter 9, you can use the project schedule and plan to set expectations and communicate with stakeholders on an ongoing basis. If you don't replan the project and communicate changes to the stakeholders when they occur, the stakeholders are left with the original expectations set at the beginning of the project—which, because the plan has changed, your team probably will not meet. The best way to keep stakeholder expectations realistic as the plan changes is to update the plan as needed and routinely share any changes with the stakeholders. This makes it much easier for your team to achieve stakeholder satisfaction.

Keeping the Right Team

Let's say that you've developed a great plan, you were given the right resources to execute it, you've developed processes that the team is actually using, and everything is going according to the plan. Don't laugh—this is possible! But line management has a tendency to take key team members off a project that's running smoothly and place them on projects that aren't going well. If these moves go unchecked, management can end up with two projects that aren't going well instead of just one.

If your project team has already developed a set of documented processes and is following them, and it's working together to identify and fix defects, you've probably made a significant investment in that team. This is especially true if your organization usually doesn't function this way; the team has gone through a cultural change to get to where it is. Cultural changes are difficult transitions to make; individuals must change their mindsets and develop new habits for performing work.

Because you've already put so much effort into your team, it is your job as the PM to guard and protect it. First, carefully analyze how changing the team's makeup will affect it before making any changes. If line management wants to remove one of your key leaders, then you must explain how the loss will affect the project plan and highlight any costs related to the change. Line managers are much more likely to listen when you connect your argument to dollars and cents.

The same careful analysis should be done when adding *new* resources to the team. Sometimes a line manager will try to place a person on your team whose skill set doesn't align with your project needs. This might be because your team has a vacancy and your manager is just trying to help, or it might be because there's nothing else for that individual to work on. In those cases, you must be prepared to say *no*. PMs have to understand that no resource is better than the wrong resource. Think about what happened on previous projects when the wrong person was assigned to your team. His or her work was probably sub-par and ended up being redone by other members of the team. Instead of paying for the work to be done once, you had to pay for it to be done twice.

Another way to protect your team is to create an environment that encourages people to want to belong to it. You can accomplish this by celebrating the team's successes and recognizing its work. If your team is executing the project plan, working together, developing high-quality products, and meeting customer expectations, it should be easy for you to find project successes to celebrate. For example, after getting a customer to sign off on one of our projects, we organized a morning of laser tag followed by a team lunch. The team loved it and appreciated being recognized for a job well done. If you cannot afford to give cash awards or pay for a team outing, you can do things that don't cost money. Take the time to write a letter of appreciation for the hard work team members have done. This positive reinforcement lets the team know that you are paying attention, and it creates incentive for the team to keep executing the plan even when times get tough.

Once you've put together the right team, you'll find that its members develop a pride of ownership in their products. They will work hard to maintain quality standards. They will also make sure that everyone follows the team processes. Once you've reached this point, your team is truly performing.

In Brief

Four techniques will help you follow the plan: creating mini-schedules, documenting and following team processes, replanning, and keeping the right team. Mini-schedules are based on inch stones, short-duration tasks that help you monitor progress and replan quickly if the project heads off track. These short-term goals help the team stay focused over the course of a long project. Documenting and following team processes fosters repeatability and consistency. If members of your team use different processes to complete the same work, your project will not be predictable, and you'll likely end up with work of inconsistent quality. Frequent replanning helps you keep the plan current. When the unforeseen happens, you must adjust the plan. This is the only way the plan will to continue to guide the work and set realistic expectations for the stakeholders. Finally, the PM can help keep the right team by protecting it from outside pressures and recognizing, appreciating, and rewarding its good work.

▓▓ Suggested Reading and Resources

Carr, Frank, with Kim Hurtado, Charles Lancaster, Charles Markert, and Paul Tucker. *Partnering in Construction: A Practical Guide to Project Success.* Chicago: American Bar Association Publishing, 1999. This excellent guide to the partnering process provides a practical approach and includes samples of the products of partnering workshops. The authors, who are professional facilitators with extensive experience in actual partnering efforts, provide lessons learned and case studies from their experience. We have personally used this process to save a major program from failure.

Doyle, Michael, and David Straus. *How To Make Meetings Work.* Berkeley Publishing, 1993. Doyle and Straus observe that most organizations spend between seven and 15 percent of their personnel budgets on meetings (this does not include the time spent preparing for meetings or attending training programs or conferences). To help readers combat waste, the authors provide a set of tools and techniques to make groups more effective. They advocate an interaction method built upon four well-defined roles: the facilitator, the recorder, the group member, and the chairperson.

Kouzes, James M., and Barry Z. Posner. *The Leadership Challenge,* 4th ed. Hoboken, NJ: John Wiley & Sons, Inc., 2007. In this book, the authors discuss how to inspire a shared vision, initiate incremental steps and small wins, foster collaboration, lead through assignments, and learn from mistakes. Understanding what makes a good leader can strengthen and improve one's leadership skills and can be applied directly to leading projects. The authors emphasize that credibility is the foundation of leadership; that successful PMs enable others to act; that a climate of trust is necessary to give power to others; and that recognizing the efforts of others is powerful.

Markert, Charles. *Partnering: Unleashing the Power of Teamwork.* Burke, VA: Mediate-Tech, Inc., 1998. For a copy, contact the author at markert@erols.com. This marketing briefing describes partnering and its attributes, characteristics, and benefits. It also provides a process for partnering, including preparing for and conducting a partnering workshop, getting feedback, and celebrating a successful effort. The briefing also presents lessons learned from real partnering experiences.

McConnell, Steve. *Software Project Survival Guide.* **Redmond, WA: Microsoft Press, 1998.** This book provides advice, suggestions, and practical help for systems or software projects. McConnell, an experienced PM, provides a project survival test that gives insight into requirements gathering, project planning, project control, risk management, and personnel management. For more information on Steve McConnell and his books, go to www.construx.com/stevemcc.

Weinberg, Gerald. *Becoming a Technical Leader: An Organic Problem-Solving Approach.* **New York: Dorset House, 1986.** This very readable book provides good advice based on the extensive experience of the author. Weinberg addresses different leadership styles and focuses on a problem-solving style generally used by successful technical leaders. See also www.geraldmweinberg.com.

Notes

1. Quantitative reports provide factual information that describes the percentage of completed work relative to the work planned for completion at that point in the schedule.
2. See Barry W. Boehm, *Software Engineering Economics* (Englewood Cliffs, NJ: Prentice Hall, 1981).
3. For an excellent description of project quality, see Dan R. Baker, "The Project Manager's Role Concerning Quality," in Ralph R. Young, *Project Requirements: A Guide to Best Practices* (Vienna, VA: Management Concepts, 2006): 141–167.

11

Managing External and Internal Expectations

Managing expectations should be straightforward. Every project has a set of objectives and requirements that it is supposed to meet, and everyone involved should understand them, especially if they have been documented. Unfortunately, this doesn't just happen. Expectations must be actively managed throughout the entire life cycle of the project. This is one of the most challenging parts of project management.

Have you ever been disappointed by a movie your friends recommended? Their rave reviews may have made you think you were about to see one of the greatest movies ever made, but the film didn't meet your sky-high expectations. If you had watched the movie with no set expectations, you would have enjoyed it and left the theater feeling satisfied. But your expectations for the movie were different from your friends'. You expected a masterpiece; they probably just expected to be entertained.

Project expectations are difficult to manage because they come from so many different places, and different groups of stakeholders have different expectations. (See Figure 1-2.) For example, your line management cares about the profit margin; your customers couldn't care less about your profit margin as long as they get what they paid for. Herein lies one of the PM's biggest challenges: working toward the profit target while satisfying customers.

▓▓ **Where Expectations Come From**

Some sources of expectations are obvious, such as documented project requirements. Some sources are much more nebulous, such as a stakeholder's invalid assumptions. For example, when we installed and configured a commercial off-the-shelf (COTS) software product, one of our stakeholders couldn't understand why the Windows-based interface of his new COTS product didn't perform search functions in the same way as the custom-developed disk operating system (DOS)-based system we were replacing. We had shown him how the COTS product performed searches before we were awarded the contract, but he still expected the new system to perform like the old one, and he complained long and loud to his management about this unmet expectation. We had to hold several meetings with him and his management team to address his concern. As you can imagine, preparing for and conducting these unplanned meetings took valuable time and resources away from working on scheduled tasks.

Expectations can come from the project's documentation. In competitive bids, this often starts with the request for proposal (RFP) that the customer puts together in preparation for soliciting proposals.[1] In the RFP, the customer does its best to describe to potential bidders the products it needs built. Depending on the skills of the person or people writing the RFP, this document can be very specific, or it can be ambiguous, leaving a lot of room for interpretation. In any case, the customer begins shaping the project's expectations as it develops the RFP.

Following the release of the RFP, potential bidders develop proposals. These proposals explain to the customer how the bidder plans to satisfy the requirements (expectations) established in the RFP. As with RFPs, some proposals are detailed, while other leave room for interpretation. After receiving the proposals, the customer establishes an evaluation team that reviews these proposals and selects the one that it feels best meets the customer's objectives. At this point, it's common for the customer's expectations to be drastically different from the bidder's expectations.

Here's an example that illustrates how this could happen. A customer put together a team of writers to develop the RFP and send it to the bidders. In preparation for receiving the bidders' proposals, the customer established a proposal evaluation team; some of the RFP writers were chosen as proposal evaluators. The winning bidder could not meet all of the RFP requirements, but it specified in the proposal which ones it couldn't meet. Meanwhile, the customer did not tell *all* of the RFP writers that the winning bidder could not satisfy all of the requirements, so some of the customer's stakeholders had expectations that were not met.

Other project documents set expectations, too. These include requirements documents, design documents, test plans, meeting minutes, project status reports, e-mails, and project presentations. If stakeholders can access a document, it can set their expectations.

The most difficult expectations to manage are those that stem from discussions. You've probably met with a customer, explained something about your project, and left the meeting confident that the customer completely understood what you said. Later, though, the customer recounts what was said differently than you remember saying it. Conversations are commonly misinterpreted and exact words forgotten. Later in this chapter, we'll discuss how meeting minutes can help manage expectations by preserving what was really said.

The expectations of internal stakeholders, such as your management team or the project team itself, also need to be actively managed throughout the life of the project. Your line management, for example, has expectations for profit margin targets and resource needs. As part of the proposal development process, most companies develop resource plans, project budgets, and profit targets, which are used to determine whether to bid on a project. These pre-proposal plans, budgets, and targets set initial management expectations that must be met for management to consider the project a success. As the PM, it is important for you to establish regular meetings with your management team throughout the life of the project to discuss these targets. Changes to the project are inevitable;

as they happen, you must discuss with management their effect on the project plans, budgets, and targets.

In Chapter 5, we discussed the importance of project teams. Many expectations come from your project team. They may include, for example, expectations about the roles each individual will play on the team or about what needs to be done to produce a project deliverable. If the project team's expectations are not properly managed, the team often has to redo work—sometimes multiple times. Imagine how this rework would affect your project's budget, schedule, and profit targets.

Team members often make assumptions about their roles on a project based on how those roles were defined on a previous project. For example, some people on one of our teams came from a project run by a different PM who had used a completely different project hierarchy. On that project, the entire team was given direction by the technical lead. This meant that the technical lead was responsible for all other team members, including technical writers and testers. On our new project, the technical lead reported to the PM; so did the test lead. We intentionally structured the project like this to maintain the independence of the product and test teams. We clearly articulated the roles and responsibilities of this organizational structure to the team so that everyone understood what was expected of them. If roles and responsibilities aren't clearly communicated, miscommunication between team members can result. Team members may neglect assignments, assuming the work is another member's responsibility.

Professional growth is related to project roles and responsibilities. Project team members often join a team expecting to expand their professional skill sets. The PM should speak with each team member to find out what his or her expectations are for the project, and then clearly communicate to that team member the type of work he or she will be assigned. If team members' expectations of professional growth are never fulfilled on the project, their morale may suffer, affecting the project. They might miss assignments, ignore team processes, or even intentionally sabotage the project.

Expectations of Different Stakeholders

Communication is the key to managing project expectations, and as the PM, ensuring effective communication is your responsibility. Think of yourself as the hub of a bicycle wheel. Each spoke of the wheel starts at the hub and leads to the rim. The rim symbolizes the project. Each spoke connecting the hub to the rim represents an expectation leading to a different stakeholder. For the wheel to be at full strength, all of the spokes have to be in place.

Communication between the stakeholders and the PM must be concise and focused on each stakeholder's specific expectations and concerns. This focused communication allows you to make the most of meetings with stakeholders—you will not waste time discussing issues and expectations they aren't interested in. The first step in identifying and building a concise communication strategy is to group the stakeholders' expectations into three related categories:

Common expectations are shared by all project stakeholders and include the project's completion date and current status. You'll discuss these with all stakeholders so that everyone gets the same message.

Internal expectations are held by the internal project and management teams. The customer or its management team would not be interested in discussing these. In fact, some internal project expectations may be proprietary information to which only authorized stakeholders should have access. These include cost information, profit status, staffing profiles, and personnel actions. The project team's management focuses on the business requirements, including profit margins, head counts, and rates of personnel use, while the project team is focused on the day-to-day activities of the project, including product capabilities and team roles and responsibilities.

External expectations are held by the customer, the customer's management team, and any other groups supporting the project (e.g., subcontractors, consultants). The customer's management team holds many of the common expectations, fulfills the customer's resource needs, and delivers the needed resources to the project at the right time. Communication with the customer's PM and his or her supporting team should focus on the customer's expectations of the products the project team is producing, the customer's needs, and the project team's and customer's schedules.

You may find that these categories of expectations don't fit your project. You'll need to figure out what your own stakeholders' concerns are. The key point is that you should determine your stakeholders' expectations at the beginning of the project so that you can develop an effective communication strategy and manage the expectations as project circumstances change.

Communicating and Managing Expectations

It's easiest to establish a method of communication with each group of stakeholders at the beginning of a project, when there aren't any problems. Most projects go through a honeymoon period, during which stakeholders are on their best behavior, trying to make a good first impression. Too often, sometime after the honeymoon period ends, some problem arises that is escalated to both the internal management team and customer's management team. The respective management teams then meet for the first time and usually play the "blame game." It will take the teams longer to resolve the problem than it should because their relationship is minimal and adversarial. It's much more effective to establish the relationships first, focus on each problem as it occurs, and resolve problems together, based on common expectations, than it is to build a "relationship" when problems crop up.[2]

To cement relationships with stakeholders, set up regularly scheduled meetings. In these meetings, you will discuss project status and set expectations. If you focus these status meetings on issues of interest to each group of stakeholders, they will find them to be informative and a productive use of their time. The number and frequency of these meetings will differ depending on your project's specific needs. For any project lasting at least six months, we schedule five kinds of status meetings:

- *Weekly meetings with the internal project team.* At these meetings, we ensure that all team members understand their roles and responsibilities and the work that must be accomplished. We also address technical issues and concerns, upcoming due dates, dependencies between tasks, and ways to improve team functioning and our products. We discuss anything of consequence that has occurred since the previous meeting. Finally, we identify potential risks and associated contingency plans.

- *Monthly project reviews with the project team's management team.* Here we cover the business goals and staffing needs of the project. We discuss the work scheduled, the work that has been produced, how the team is doing in relation to our business goals, and any potential risks and risk-mitigation strategies. Candid discussions where managers can offer suggestions or provide assistance are the most helpful. If we provide only the good news, no really helpful information is likely to be shared.

- *Quarterly management reviews with the project team's senior management.* The subject matter is similar to what's covered in the monthly project reviews with the management team, though it is often less detailed.

- *Weekly status meetings with the customer's project team.* Here we meet with the customer stakeholders who work on the project day-to-day. We review the project's status as well as upcoming deliverables, highlighting any customer due dates and dependencies. We also review any project risks and associated mitigation strategies. The customer may "own" certain risks and must be aware of those risks and have contingency plans in place if they come to fruition. This is an ongoing opportunity to further strengthen and improve communications.

- *Monthly project reviews with the project team's management and customer's management.* Here the PM brings together both sets of management teams to review project status and discuss potential problems. These meetings are initially intended to establish good rapport between the management teams during the honeymoon period and later serve as a mechanism to collectively identify and resolve issues.

Before conducting each type of meeting for the first time, we review with each stakeholder group the meeting agenda and goals. Specifically, we articulate to the group what we plan to cover and solicit feedback from the group so that we can adjust the agenda accordingly. We continue to solicit input between meetings by asking the stakeholders if they would like to add additional information to the agenda or if there are topics that they'd prefer not be covered.

Stakeholders' expectations can differ significantly after reading project documentation like the RFP, proposal, and SOW. These regular status meetings help you clarify any ambiguity. They're an opportunity to communicate, document, and manage expectations from the beginning of the project and as they change. Regular meetings facilitate managing expectations, which is of the most challenging project responsibilities.

You're probably thinking that all of these meetings will require a lot of time and effort. Actually, each meeting should take only about one hour. If you follow the schedule we outlined, you will spend two hours a week in status meetings with both the internal and external day-to-day project teams; two hours a month meeting with both sets of management teams; and an additional hour once a quarter to meet with your own senior management team. This is a reasonable cost considering the benefits these meetings provide.

Meeting Minutes

Meeting minutes document the topics covered and project decisions made during a meeting. The meeting minutes are then delivered to and approved by the meeting attendees. The attendees should review the minutes to make sure everyone is "on the same page." The minutes may help resolve miscommunications.

Meeting minutes must be timely. All parties should agree on a reasonable turnaround time. For most of our projects, we require that the meeting minutes be produced within three days of the meeting; the customer then has three days after receiving the minutes to provide updates or clarifications. The turnaround time should be agreed to by all parties and then strictly adhered to throughout the life of the project.

Meeting minutes take about the same amount of time to write up as the meeting lasted, so for a one-hour meeting you can expect to spend about one hour writing the minutes. One of our managers actually wrote meeting minutes *before* meetings. We wondered how this was possible, but she told us that because she was leading the meetings, she knew what she was going to cover and could write it out ahead of time. After each meeting, she spent about 10 or 15 minutes adding in any additional topics that were discussed.

Writing the minutes before the meeting helps you more thoroughly prepare for each meeting by forcing you to write down all of the topics you planned to cover and the expectations you want to set. It enables you to deliver the meeting minutes faster, typically on the same day as the meeting, and you'll be able to obtain approval more quickly. It also allows attendees to review the meeting while it's still fresh in everyone's mind.

Another approach is to review the minutes of the previous meeting just prior to the next meeting. This will refresh your memory on important follow-up items.

Meeting minutes are valuable—and often under-utilized—tools that foster effective communication.

In Brief

Managing expectations is one of the most challenging but most critical aspects of project management. When a stakeholder's expectations are too high, and you fail to meet them, the project is a failure from his or her point of view. Stakeholder expectations must be actively managed throughout the project. Expectations are constantly changing, based on design decisions, meetings, informal conversations, and other factors. When protocols for communication, such as regularly scheduled meetings, are established very early in the project, these expectations can be clearly communicated, documented, and managed.

Suggested Reading and Resources

Covey, Stephen R. *The 8th Habit: From Effectiveness to Greatness.* **New York: Free Press, 2004.** In this book, Stephen Covey tells readers how to achieve results in all aspects of their lives by providing the principles of personal and organizational leadership that create trust, commitment, and fulfillment. Covey states that ambiguous or broken expectations are the root cause of almost all communications breakdowns, and that clarifying roles and defining high-priority goals will facilitate communications. Covey provides an interesting analysis of the differences between leadership and management, and concludes that both are vital—one without the other is insufficient.

Humphrey, Watts S. "Why Don't They Practice What We Preach?" Available online at www.sei.cmu.edu/publications/articles/practice-preach/practice-preach.html. This insightful article describes why technical professionals do not use optimal methods to achieve results, even when there is clear evidence supporting one particular method or another. Regardless of their experience and training, engineers tend to stick to the practices they are familiar with, and they require a considerable amount of evidence before trying a new approach to a problem. Today's organizations have few role models that consistently demonstrate effective work habits and discipline, which accounts partially for industry deliverables that have not improved in spite of dramatic improvements in practices, methods, techniques, and tools. Steve McConnell's *After the Gold Rush: Creating a*

True Profession of Software Engineering is full of ideas and suggestions for developing the engineering profession.

Porter-Roth, Bud. *Request for Proposal: A Guide to Effective RFP Development*. Boston, MA: Addison-Wesley, 2002. An RFP is a standard tool used by governments and businesses to purchase products and services by promoting competitive proposals among suppliers. The author provides a comprehensive guidebook that addresses all aspects of the RFP process. He believes the RFP process rarely receives the attention it deserves, and yet it serves as a foundation for any successful project by clarifying intended deliverables before the project starts. The book provides practical advice and suggestions for each section of the RFP, templates for many sections, and examples of both effective and poorly written RFPs.

Notes

1. See Bud Porter-Roth, *Request for Proposal: A Guide to Effective RFP Development* (Boston: Addison-Wesley, 2002), for an explanation of the RFP process.
2. Establishing good relationships at the beginning of the project is one of the benefits of the partnering process described in Chapter 10. See the suggested reading on that subject at the end of that chapter.

12 Managing Scope

Managing the scope of a project causes project teams more difficulty than any other part of the project. It cannot be avoided because requirements will inevitably change during the life cycle of the project.

The average project invests three percent of total costs in the project-long requirements process, but data from NASA show that much better results are achieved when eight to 14 percent of total project costs are invested in the requirements process.[1] This chapter will give you insight into several best practices that you can implement rather easily to manage the scope of your project:

- Defining the requirements
- Evolving the real requirements
- Prioritizing requirements
- Tracing requirements
- Managing requirements.

Many books on requirements are available; we recommend that you take the time to read two or three of those noted in Figure 12-1. Not only should *you* become familiar with the requirements process, but you should also mentor all members of your project, including your requirements manager or requirements analyst (RA). Use Figure 12-2 to determine the skills your RA must have, and suggest books, professional

FIGURE 12-1: Requirements-Related Books for PMs

Please see References at the end of this book for publication information.	
Effective Requirements Practices	Describes *what* to do on a project from a requirements perspective. Written for the PM and the requirements analyst (RA).
The Requirements Engineering Handbook	Describes *how* to perform requirements-related work. Written for the RA or requirements manager.
Project Requirements: A Guide To Best Practices	Provides a set of recommended best practices. Written for the PM to help him or her understand the *value* of requirements-related activities and *how* to perform them.
Performance-Based Earned Value	Illustrates a requirements-based approach for performing earned-value management techniques on a project. In other words, provide an earned value approach that is worthwhile.
Writing Better Requirements	Explains how to write good requirements.
Customer-Centered Products: Creating Successful Products through Smart Requirements Management	Offers a customer-based approach that can be connected to project requirements.
Managing Software Requirements: A Unified Approach	Provides a detailed discussion of many requirements elicitation methods and techniques.

development courses, or conferences to him or her that will facilitate personal growth and development and that offer information needed for your project.[2]

The requirements are the basis for all of the other work that is done on the project. As noted previously, there is always pressure to get going on the "real work," but you should resist initiating other technical work until your customer, users, and project team are satisfied that you have a good set of *real* requirements. This will help provide a foundation for project success.

Defining the Requirements

Customers and users provide what we call *stated requirements,* the requirements given at the beginning of a system- or software-development effort. Of course, the stated requirements are *never* the real requirements. Customers and users need help to analyze the stated requirements and

FIGURE 12-2: Requirements Analyst Skills Matrix

> **KEY**
> **Knowledge of = K   Experience with = X**
> **REH:** Ralph R. Young, *The Requirements Engineering Handbook* (Boston: Artech House, 2004).
> **ERP:** Ralph R. Young, *Effective Requirements Practices* (Boston: Addison-Wesley, 2001).
> **WBR:** Ian F. Alexander and Richard Stevens, *Writing Better Requirements* (London: Addison-Wesley, 2002).
> **SL:** Soren Lauesen, *Software Requirements: Styles and Techniques* (Reading, MA: Addison-Wesley, 2002): 346–347.
> **EG1:** Ellen Gottesdiener, *Requirements by Collaboration: Workshops for Defining Needs* (New York: Addison-Wesley, 2002): 122–128.
> **EG2:** Ibid., 89–94.
> **Gilb:** Visit www.gilb.com and insert "impact estimation" in the search feature.

Line No.	Requirements Analyst Skills	References	Entry/ Junior-Level Analyst	Mid-Level Analyst	Senior-Level Analyst
1.	Types of requirements	**REH, Ch 4**	K	X	X
2.	Criteria for a good requirement	**REH, Ch 1**	K	X	X
3.	Customer/user involvement with requirements joint team	**ERP, Ch 3**	K	X	X
4.	Evolving real requirements from the stated requirements	**ERP, Ch 4**	K	X	X
5.	Anticipating and controlling requirements changes	**REH, Ch 1**	K	X	X
6.	Office automation tools	**Tutorials**	X	X	X
7.	References concerning requirements (books, articles, standards)	**Bibliography ERP, REH**	K	X	X
8.	Requirements attributes	**REH, Ch 5**	K	X	X
9.	Requirements baseline	**REH, Ch 6**	K	X	X
10.	Training in systems engineering (e.g., life cycles, risk management)	**REH, Ch 5**	K	X	X
11.	Requirements justification/rationale	**REH, Ch 5**	K	X	X
12.	Requirements management tools (e.g., DOORS, RequisitePro)	**REH, Ch 5**	K	X	X
13.	Requirements peer review/inspection/ walk-through	**REH, Ch 5**	K	X	X
14.	Requirements syntax	**WBR, Ch 7**	K	X	X
15.	Requirements traceability	**REH, Ch 5**	K	X	X
16.	Requirements verification and validation (V&V)	**ERP, Ch 9**	K	X	X

Line No.	Requirements Analyst Skills	References	Entry/ Junior-Level Analyst	Mid-Level Analyst	Senior-Level Analyst
17.	System/subsystem/software-level requirements	REH, Ch 5	K	X	X
18.	Developing and using metrics for requirements activities/processes	REH, Ch 2	K	X	X
19.	Technical writing of requirements deliverables (requirements traceability matrix (RTM), software requirements specification (SRS), interface requirements specification (IRS)	REH, Ch 4	K	X	X
20.	Develop, implement, and use requirements processes	ERP, Ch 5		K	X
21.	Familiarity with Microsoft Project	Tutorial		K	X
22.	Quality assurance (QA) process for requirements	REH, Ch 9		K	X
23.	Requirements allocation (to components, applications, and packages)	REH, Ch 4		K	X
24.	Requirements change control and change notification	ERP, Ch 10		K	X
25.	Requirements repository	REH, Ch 5		K	X
26.	Requirements errors (missing, incorrect, unfeasible, out of scope)	REH, Ch 6		K	X
27.	Requirements defect notification	REH, Ch 6		K	X
28.	Requirements dissemination to customers/users/developers/testers	REH, Ch 4		K	X
29.	Requirements elicitation	REH, Ch 5		K	X
30.	Requirements identification	REH, Ch 5		K	X
31.	Use case development (with customer/ user and based on user's guides)	REH, Ch 7		K	X
32.	Requirements in customer/user decision making process	REH, Ch 1		K	X
33.	Requirements interaction with CM	REH, Ch 6		X	X
34.	Requirements negotiation	SL, EG1		X	X
35.	Requirements ownership	WBR, EG2		X	X
36.	Requirements prioritization	REH, Ch 5		X	X
37.	Requirements review board (RRB)/ configuration review board (CRB)/ configuration control board (CCB)	REH, Ch 7		X	X
38.	Requirements rough order of magnitude (ROM) costs	REH, Ch 7		X	X
39.	Requirements specifications	REH, Ch 7		X	X

Line No.	Requirements Analyst Skills	References	Entry/ Junior- Level Analyst	Mid- Level Analyst	Senior- Level Analyst
40.	Evaluating requirements for risks	**REH, Ch 7**			X
41.	Training the project team in the requirements processes	**REH, Ch 5**			X
42.	Requirements impact estimation (IE) table	**Gilb**			K

Reproduced by permission from Artech House, Norwood, MA, from *The Requirements Engineering Handbook* by Ralph Young, published 2004.

---

evolve the real requirements. The reason for this is that each stakeholder (anyone who has an interest in the success or failure[3] of a project) has a different perspective on the requirements. It's vital to involve all stakeholders in the development of a vision and scope document and the high-level system requirements.

Best practices for defining the requirements include:

- Writing a vision and scope document
- Establishing a joint team
- Using better requirements elicitation methods and techniques
- Ensuring that every requirement meets the criteria for a good requirement
- Identifying the rationale for each requirement
- Using an appropriate automated requirements tool
- Ensuring that each requirement is testable
- Employing measurement in the requirements work.

Writing a Vision and Scope Document

Writing a vision and scope document allows you to thoughtfully consider the goals and objectives of a project. Share this document with various groups of stakeholders to get feedback, which can help clarify the real intent of the project. An excellent template for the vision and scope document developed by Karl Wiegers is provided as Appendix C in Ralph Young's book *Project Requirements: A Guide to Best Practices*.

Establishing a Joint Team

A joint team is composed of up to 20 people (or more, depending on the size of the project) from both the customer/user stakeholder and the developer stakeholder. It has the following responsibilities:

- Reviewing the stated requirements and evolving the real requirements for the project

- Prioritizing the requirements

- Considering all new requirements and all changes to requirements and deciding how they will be dealt with, preferably using techniques that help manage change, such as new products, versions, releases, and baselines.

The joint team provides an analytical review and acts as a funnel for changes, which helps control the requirements. Members of the joint team should be empowered to make binding decisions.

Using Better Requirements Elicitation Methods and Techniques

Of the almost 40 existing requirements elicitation methods and techniques, these have proven to be the most effective (a discussion of each of these is provided in *The Requirements Engineering Handbook*[4]):

- Interviews

- Document analysis

- Brainstorming

- Requirements workshops

- Prototyping

- Use cases

- Storyboards

- Interfaces analysis

- Modeling

- Performance and capacity analysis.

During requirements elicitation, the focus should be on product benefits, not on having as many features as possible. (The Standish Group has concluded from its research that 45 percent of the features provided in most delivered systems are never used at all![5]) Think of the time, effort, cost, and confusion your project can save by evolving the real requirements.

Ensuring That Every Requirement Meets the Criteria for a Good Requirement

Often, work needs to be redone because many requirements are poorly elucidated. Their flaws are discovered late in the development process and prove to be extremely costly. This problem can be overcome by evaluating each requirement by the criteria illustrated in Figure 12-3. These criteria should be included as one of the attributes in the project's automated requirements tool. This will remind developers to verify that these criteria are met for every requirement.

Identifying the Rationale for Each Requirement

Industry requirements trainer and consultant Ivy Hooks found while working at NASA that after she asked why each requirement on a given project was needed, she could eliminate half of the requirements! Your joint team should discuss and analyze all of the requirements to determine which ones aren't necessary. This step can significantly reduce the effort, time, and money spent on a project. It will also identify some low-priority requirements that could perhaps be addressed in a subsequent

FIGURE 12-3: The Criteria for a Good Requirement

Each requirement should be:
- **Necessary.** If the system can meet prioritized real needs without the requirement, it isn't necessary.
- **Feasible.** The requirement can be fulfilled without going over budget and within the time allotted in the schedule.
- **Correct.** The facts related to the requirement are accurate, and it is technically and legally possible to implement it.
- **Concise.** The requirement is stated simply.
- **Unambiguous.** The requirement can be interpreted in only one way.
- **Complete.** All conditions under which the requirement applies are stated, and each requirement expresses a whole idea or statement.
- **Consistent.** Does not conflict with other requirements.
- **Verifiable.** Implementation of the requirement in the system can be proven.
- **Traceable.** One can trace back to the source of the requirement, and it can also be tracked throughout the system (i.e., through design, code, test, and documentation).
- **Allocated.** The requirement is assigned to a component of the designed system.
- **Design-independent.** Does not pose a specific implementation solution.
- **Non-redundant.**
- **Devoid** of escape clauses such as *if, when, but, except, unless,* and *although;* not speculative or general (avoid wording such as *usually, generally, often, normally,* and *typically*).

Also, each requirement:
- Should have a unique identifying number.
- Should be stated as an imperative using shall.

Reproduced by permission from Artech House, Norwood, MA, from The Requirements Engineering Handbook by Ralph Young, published 2004.

---

release. Anything that can be done to reduce complexity, eliminate unnecessary requirements, and defer low-priority requirements will enhance your ability to complete the project successfully.

Using an Automated Requirements Tool

We assert that an industry-strength automated requirements tool should be used for all projects, except tiny ones.[6] There are several reasons for this:

- Many attributes of each requirement must be tracked

- Each requirement must be traceable, from its source to its products (and vice versa), through all phases of the project

- Data concerning the requirements is volatile and must be tracked.

This enables developers to track where each requirement is met in the design, the software, in testing, and in documentation (e.g., in the user manual).

Ensuring That Each Requirement Is Testable

We recommend involving testers in the requirements development process to confirm that each requirement is testable. Most projects spend far too much time and money on testing because teams do not discover that many requirements are not testable until very late in the project development process, necessitating a lot of rework. (The industry average for rework on a project is 45 percent. By reducing expensive, time-consuming rework, you can instead spend money and time on investing in proven best practices, defining and deploying processes, and conducting measurement activities and requirements activities.)

Employing Measurement in Requirements Work

We recommend employing measurement in the project's requirements work in two ways:

- Ensure that each requirement is measurable.

- Quantify the whole set of requirements: the total number of requirements, the number of requirements approved, the number rejected, the number under consideration, and requirements volatility (the amount of change to the requirements). It's vital to track these data to control the project.

Evolving the Real Requirements

To ensure project success, the PM should require the entire project team, including customers, users, designers, developers, subcontractors, and consultants, to work on evolving the real requirements. Identifying the real requirements helps the project team:

- Meet budget and schedule

- Produce products and work of high quality

- Minimize rework

- Significantly reduce risk.

We selected the word *evolve* carefully. Figuring out the real requirements that lay the foundation for your entire project is not simply a matter of identifying—or "gathering"—the requirements. You must consider all of the stated requirements, elicit those that have not been stated, and evolve a set of prioritized requirements that best support the vision and scope document and are within the cost, schedule, and quality objectives of your project. Best practices you can use to evolve the real requirements include:

- *Recruiting an effective requirements analyst.* Industry trainer and expert Robert Halligan believes that this should be the PM's most important consideration and that most projects are in jeopardy because they lack a competent RA. (The RA's skills are described in Figure 12-2.)

- *Identifying all stakeholders.* Failing to identify an important stakeholder can jeopardize the project—even if it is near successful completion.

- *Performing careful requirements analysis.* Requirements analysis is not a simple, straightforward discipline.[7] It is an organized method used to understand the aspects—or "attributes"—of each requirement. A requirement's attributes include its origin, priority, cost, relative difficulty to achieve, location in the system, and author, and the attributes also describe any revisions to the requirement, the date those revisions were made, and a description of where the revisions are documented.[8]

- ***Perform trade studies as needed.*** A *trade study* is an analysis of alternative courses of action in which a balancing of factors that are not attainable at the same time is performed. Whenever there are multiple viable alternatives, a trade study can be used to identify the best approach.

- ***Ensure good communication*** with customers and users and among the project's staff.

- ***Write good requirements.*** Requirements must be expressed in a way that users of the planned system can understand. A good requirement is unambiguous; uses a limited and commonly understood vocabulary; is stated in simple, direct sentences; identifies the type of user who states the requirement; and provides criteria to use to determine whether the requirement has been fulfilled.

Prioritizing Requirements

Not all requirements are of equal importance, and some are easier than others to implement in a project, system, or software development effort. We often do—but should *not*—treat all requirements as more or less of the same priority. Invest in your project's requirements process by assigning each requirement a priority based on its importance relative to all other requirements and to the goals, objectives, vision, and scope of the project. Figure 12-4 explains why this is important. You will most likely be able to eliminate many lowest-priority requirements, or at least postpone them for later delivery. The RA, designers, and developers can then meet to assess the relative difficulty of implementing each requirement. Levels of difficulty might be "high," "medium," "easy," and "no-brainer."

There are also various types of requirements.[9] For example, *high-level requirements* are the major functional capabilities that must be built into a system to meet its stakeholders' needs. There might be 50 to 200

FIGURE 12-4: Prioritizing Requirements

Why is it important to prioritize requirements?
- We assume, incorrectly, that all requirements are of equal importance and urgency.
- Systems can't do everything for everyone, and we should not try to build them to do so.
- We don't understand that we should simply meet minimum requirements; anything more is too much.
- We don't have enough time and money to do everything.
- We must fulfill high quality objectives in everything we do.

What can we do?
- Use the joint team mechanism to prioritize all requirements.
- Agree to address top-priority requirements in the first baseline, release, or version.
- Agree to address lower-priority requirements in subsequent baselines, releases, or versions.
- Agree not to include low-priority requirements within the scope of the system, if possible.

high-level requirements for a project, system, or software development effort, depending on the size and scope of the system. Identifying the high-level requirements enables the project team, customers, and all other stakeholders to determine the most important goals, objectives, and work products of the system to be delivered. Using this approach, the team can avoid getting so enmeshed in detailed requirements that it loses control of the project. It's very important to include these high-level requirements in your automated requirements tool.

Tracing Requirements

In our experience, many PMs are not familiar with requirements tracing and do not know why it is so important; many RAs do not understand it or know how to do it. The best guidance available on this topic was written by James D. Palmer and can be found in Appendix A in *Project Requirements: A Guide to Best Practices.*[10]

Requirements traceability means that it is essential to know how each requirement is or will be addressed in every phase of the project, from its source (the person who suggested or nominated the requirement; the RA must know with whom to talk about each requirement) onward—to the requirements document, to design, to development, to testing, to documentation, and to training.

Further, bidirectional traceability is required by the industry standard Capability Maturity Model® Integration (CMMI); you must be able to trace requirements both forward and backward (from testing, to development, to the design, to the requirements document, to the source of the requirement). The motivation for traceability differs for the two directions: forward—to determine whether the requirement is adequately covered by the design, in testing, and in documentation; backward—to determine if the design and the tests are really needed to meet requirements.

Managing Requirements

The most common reason projects fail is failure to evolve the real requirements. The second most common reason is failure to manage new requirements and changes to requirements. Projects get out of control when changes to the initially stated requirements are frequent and continuous and when stakeholders insist on adding new requirements without reason or thought. This is a recipe for disaster!

Some methods of managing scope creep include:[11]

- Maintain a control point in the project, to whom everyone provides all requests for changes in requirements. This person is typically the requirements manager, requirements engineer, or requirements analyst.

- Ensure that all members of the project team are aware that they cannot accept, approve, or implement changes in requirements independently or without project approval.

- Determine the cost and schedule impact of each requested change, and present that information when submitting a change request for approval.

- Limit the percentage of requirements changes—often referred to as the level of "requirements volatility"—to 0.5 percent per month.

Anything more can jeopardize the team's ability to maintain control of the project.

Figure 12-5 shows that during the development process, we should work to continually improve customer and producer (developer) understanding and interpretation of requirements. We can collaboratively develop a better understanding by conducting requirements reviews and design reviews, and by developing prototypes, performing acceptance testing, and providing change requests. Through work activities, the recommendations of customers and developers become more commonly understood.

FIGURE 12-5: Improve Understanding and Interpretation of Requirements During the Development Process

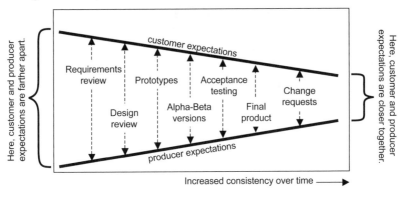

In Brief

Because project requirements will change during the project's life cycle, the PM must determine how to manage the scope of the project. Begin by resisting the pressure to get going prematurely on the "real work." Do not perform other technical work until you have a good set of real requirements. This will prevent rework and wasted resources.

Best practices for defining the real requirements are writing a vision and scope document, establishing a joint team, using better requirements elicitation methods and techniques, ensuring that every requirement meets the criteria for a good requirement, identifying the rationale for each requirement, using an industry-strength automated requirements tool, ensuring that each requirement is testable, and employing measurement in the requirements work.

Remember that not all requirements are of equal importance, nor do they require equal effort to implement. Determine the importance of each requirement and estimate the relative difficulty of implementing it. Tackle the most difficult requirements early. Make sure that all requirements are traceable back to their source, and know how they'll be addressed in every phase of the project. Finally, careful management of new requirements and changes to requirements is essential to maintaining control of the project and its success.

Suggested Reading and Resources

Alexander, Ian F., and Richard Stevens. *Writing Better Requirements.* London: Addison-Wesley, 2002. This book offers guidance on writing good requirements from experienced authors committed to improving industry experience. Unfortunately, requirements for systems and software are typically underdeveloped. This book explains in a nontechnical way how to elicit requirements from users, how to organize them in a way that technical staff can understand them, and how to review requirements at every stage of the project. The authors provide helpful guidance about requirements writing that will help readers avoid typical problems, and they provide exercises and answers that offer insight into 18 requirements development techniques.

Capability Maturity Model Integration (CMMI) Project. The CMMI project is a collaborative effort sponsored by the U.S. Department of Defense, Office of the Secretary of Defense for Acquisition, Technology, and Logistics, and the National Defense Industrial Association, with participation by government, industry, and the Software Engineering Institute. The project's objective is to develop a product suite that provides industry and government with a set of integrated products to support process and product improvement. The intent is to preserve government and industry investment in process improvement and enhance the use of multiple models. The project's outputs will be integrated models, assessment methods, and training materials. For more information about CMMI, see www.sei". cmu.edu/cmmi/general.

Hooks, Ivy F. "Guide for Managing and Writing Requirements." 1994. Available from ivyh@complianceautomation.com. This concise, well-written guidebook is based on the extensive experience of a practicing requirements engineer and consultant. It addresses scoping a project, managing requirements, and writing good requirements, as well as systems organization, levels of requirements, requirements attributes, and specifications.

Hooks, Ivy F. "Managing Requirements." Available online at the Compliance Automation website, www.complianceautomation.com. This article provides a good analysis of how failing to invest in the requirements process affects projects, and it describes the major problems the author has witnessed during her experiences as a requirements engineer. The article also describes some of the characteristics of good requirements.

Hooks, Ivy F. "Writing Good Requirements: A One-Day Tutorial." Sponsored by the Washington Metropolitan Area Chapter of the International Council on Systems Engineering, June 1997. This briefing and course can help a project or an organization in dealing with the requirements process. The pearl here is to ensure that you have a requirements process and that you take advantage of industry best practices in executing it. Don't attempt to find your own way at considerable financial, personal, project, and organizational costs.

Hossenlopp, Rosemary, and Kathleen B. Hass. *Unearthing Business Requirements: Elicitation Tools and Techniques.* **Vienna, VA: Management Concepts, 2008.** This new book is an informative and helpful companion to the information about requirements elicitation provided in our book. The authors provide practical, detailed, and complete guidance for all aspects of the elicitation process. Chapter 5, "Determine the Project Life Cycle," is particularly useful because this critical step is often skipped because managers don't realize that requirements activities—their sequence, timing, and deliverables—differ according to the project life cycle.

Chapter 8, "Requirements Elicitation Workshops and Discovery Sessions," is also very useful. We strongly recommend incorporating requirements workshops into the project. This chapter describes different types of requirements workshops, along with rules, tips, and advice for tailoring a workshop to suit a particular project. The book also provides templates for the business requirements document and the requirements management plan, and a terrific graphic describes requirements development and requirements management artifacts.

Leffingwell, Dean, and Don Widrig. *Managing Software Requirements: A Unified Approach.* **Reading, MA: Addison-Wesley, 2000.** Emphasizes the team skills that help ensure that a project's requirements process works. The authors describe proven techniques for understanding needs, organizing requirements information, and managing the scope of a project. The book also provides an insightful description of most requirements elicitation techniques.

McConnell, Steve. *After the Gold Rush: Creating a True Profession of Software Engineering.* **Redmond, Washington: Microsoft, 1999.** McConnell's easy-to-read style prevails in this excellent analysis of the status of software engineering today. He places the state of current practices into context and notes that each of us has a choice: to maintain "code-and-fix" development practices or boldly venture toward a true profession.

Russell, Lou, and Jeff Feldman. *IT Leadership Alchemy.* **Upper Saddle River, NJ: Prentice Hall PTR, 2003.** This book is aimed at helping the PM by addressing the human and business skills needed to manage projects. It offers managers advice on dealing with change in a complex environment, identifies the core relationship-management skills, and provides templates, checklists, assessment tools, and scenarios from the authors' experience.

Notes

1. Ivy F. Hooks, *Guide for Managing and Writing Requirements* (Boerne, TX: Compliance Automation, 1994).

2. The old adage "no one learns more than the teacher" is true. As a proactive mechanism to improve communications on your project, consider asking your staff to periodically make presentations to one another about what's new in their area of responsibility. Consider also encouraging your staff to make presentations and teach tutorials and workshops at conferences.

3. Be aware that there may be negative stakeholders associated with your project. A negative stakeholder is someone who is not an advocate for the project or who actively works against the project's objectives. For example, users of an existing system may not advocate its replacement.

4. Ralph R. Young, *The Requirements Engineering Handbook* (Boston: Addison-Wesley, 2001).

5. The Standish Group, "What Are Your Requirements?" (West Yarmouth, MA: The Standish Group International, 2003).

6. A tiny project may be defined as one supported by two to four developers and lasting less than six months.

7. See Ralph Young, *Effective Requirements Practices* (Boston: Addison-Wesley, 2001), for a description of 14 aspects of the requirements process.

8. Ibid., 87. Also, Chapter 4 of the same text provides specific recommendations to use to determine the requirements for a planned system.

9. For a comprehensive discussion of the types of requirements, see Chapter 4 in Ralph R. Young, *The Requirements Engineering Handbook* (Boston: Addison-Wesley, 2001).

10. See Appendix A, "Traceability," in *Project Requirements: A Guide to Best Practices* (Vienna, VA: Management Concepts, 2006): 201–222.

11. See Chapter 10 of *Effective Requirements Practices* for a recommended approach to issues stemming from requirements volatility.

13 Managing Quality

One of your goals as a PM is to build quality into work products, rather than trying to add quality to work products near the end of the project. The essence of this approach is to plan in quality from the beginning of the project. Surface any problems early and correct them as soon as possible, maintain your plan, and minimize rework. This chapter provides a road map for building quality into your project's work products. This approach reduces cost and improves schedule adherence, which satisfies users and customers and helps your team meet all stakeholders' criteria for project success (as described in Figure 1-2).

Quality can be improved by changing the processes used on the project. This sounds like common sense, but most project teams are consumed with charging ahead and do not bother to create effective processes and continually improve them. Poor project results do *not* reflect the competency and industriousness of the individuals who worked on the project. They stem from using ineffective processes.

What Is Quality?

We begin by defining some terms related to quality. The definitions we provide may not be ones you're familiar with, but we consider them useful and effective working definitions.

- *Quality* products can be defined as those meeting real customer needs. Recall from Figure 1-2 that *all* stakeholders consider (or *should* consider) quality an important criterion.

- *Quality assurance (QA)* is a process in which policies, processes, and work results are independently evaluated and management is given feedback.

- *Quality control (QC)* ensures that work products meet specified criteria.

- *Quality management (QM)* may be defined as integrating practices to build continuous improvement into a work approach.

- A project team or organization with a strong *quality culture* works toward continuous improvement and customer satisfaction. Employees value quality and take active steps in their daily work to improve and achieve quality.

- *Quantitative management (QM)* involves basing decisions on data.

In this chapter, we describe mechanisms for building quality into work products, including process orientation, quality control audits, peer reviews and inspections, defect prevention, and QM. Managing quality is the responsibility of the program or project manager (PM). The PM should emphasize the importance and value of establishing and maintaining a quality culture on the project. He or she can reinforce this vital attitude through daily communications, during regular meetings and brown-bag events, and by using the project approach we advocate in this book.

- *Process orientation:* Having a process orientation suggests that processes for work activities are defined, used, and continuously improved. These processes include project planning, configuration management, requirements development and management, defect prevention, quality assurance, training, and technology change management, among others. A good framework that provides the needed practices for each process area (PA) is the Capability Maturity Model Integration (CMMI). It can be downloaded from the Software Engineering Institute (SEI) website, www.sei.cmu.edu/cmmi. We encourage you to use this framework or another one.[1]

- An experienced and trained **QA manager** can make an enormous difference on every project. In Chapter 10 of Ralph Young's *Project Requirements: A Guide to Best Practices*, a seasoned and successful QA manager, Dan Baker, describes the role of QA in depth and explains how to effectively perform this critical role. This is the best description we've found of the QA manager's role.

- *Managing scope:* As we discussed in the previous chapter, allowing requirements creep (uncontrolled scope growth) is a common cause of projects getting out of control. The quality of the implemented system can be (and often is) jeopardized by the failure to control requirements creep.

- *Performing effective project planning and tracking:* This is one of this book's key messages. Project teams rarely plan effectively. It's vital to think through the internal and external work products that are required and to estimate the time and effort that will be required to create them. It's also critical to create a plan and continually update it.

Planning for Quality: Quality Control Audits

Performing effective QA involves much more than reviewing documents. Quality control audits are one of the most effective mechanisms to make sure project work is done correctly. Quality control audits are performed throughout the project. The audit is a review by someone in the QA organization. QA evaluates the way the work processes are performed and compares them to the project's documented processes. It identifies shortcomings in how the processes are actually used (Figure 13-1).

A Plan-Do-Check-Act (PDCA) cycle, as described in Figure 13-2, should be used for all project activities (e.g., at the end of meetings, at

FIGURE 13-1: How the Components of a Quality Management Approach Work Together

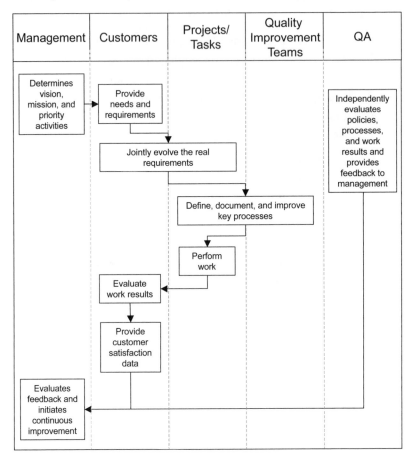

Reproduced by permission from Artech House, Norwood, MA, from *The Requirements Engineering Handbook* by Ralph Young, published 2004.

project milestones, at the end of a project). PDCA should be performed by groups at the end of all meetings. The idea is to plan the approach, implement (do) it, check on how things are working, act on the results of that checking, and continue the continuous improvement cycle.

FIGURE 13-2: The Plan-Do-Check-Act (PDCA) Cycle

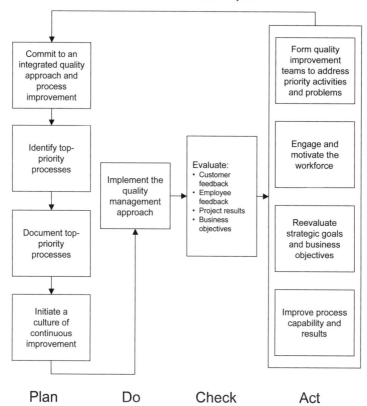

Reproduced by permission from Artech House, Norwood, MA, from *The Requirements Engineering Handbook* by Ralph Young, published 2004.

We also "do PDCA," to use the term loosely, during the last 10 minutes of our meetings. We give each person at the meeting the chance to suggest how meetings could be made better or how we might make other improvements. This technique really works. One person's idea often sparks an idea from another, and improvements are born.

▒▒ **Peer Reviews and Inspections**

Peer reviews are among the most powerful project processes. A *peer review* is an activity in which one or more persons who are not the author or creator of a work product examine that product with the intent of finding defects and improvement opportunities.[2] An *inspection* is a more rigorous type of peer review.[3] As in a standard peer review, people other than the author or creator of the work product examine that product with the intent of finding defects and improvement opportunities. Inspections may incorporate sampling (the process or technique of selecting a representative part of a population to determine the characteristic of the entire population).[4]

Perhaps the most useful, definitive treatment of this topic is provided by Karl Wiegers in *Peer Reviews in Software: A Practical Guide*. The peer review process area in the Capability Maturity Model® for Software (SW-CMM) also is helpful in defining or tailoring a peer review process.[5] The SW-CMM can be downloaded from the SEI website at www.sei.cmu.edu.

Peer reviews and inspections are particularly valuable because they enable others to conceive of and suggest improvement opportunities. They also allow the team to find defects in the work products early in the product development process. Remember that the earlier a defect or error is discovered:

- The easier it is to fix

- The less impact it will have on other work products and the project as a whole

- The less it will cost, and time it will take, to get back on track.

Peer reviews and inspections allow others working on the project—peers—to become more familiar with the project's approach and work products. They help ensure that team members are supporting each other and working toward the same goals.[6]

All project staff should be trained in performing peer reviews and inspections effectively. Those leading peer reviews and inspections should be trained in peer review facilitation.[7] Effective peer reviews make a major contribution to the project's goals and objectives, but if they're performed incorrectly or inefficiently, they can waste time and effort.

An effective peer review is one that efficiently identifies errors or defects and provides the author the opportunity to improve the work product. If an organization or project finds itself experiencing ineffective peer reviews, training should be provided for all those involved in the peer review process.

Defect Prevention

Defect prevention (DP) (or causal analysis and resolution [CAR], as it is called in the CMMI), should be performed for *all* projects. DP is the use of technologies and techniques (for example, root cause analysis) that minimize the risk of making errors in work products, including deliverables. It enables the project team to address directly the problems it is experiencing.

Let's consider a sample DP process, as shown in Figure 13-3. Your project might begin with this process; later, you can add additional components you deem necessary, such as metrics to evaluate the effectiveness of the process, a DP plan, or a DP repository.

The first step is to identify a work product or process that is creating problems ("points of pain") for the project. For example, a team might believe that an ineffective requirements approach is to blame for project problems. The team will then evaluate the project's requirements process. If the process is not documented, a few interested and motivated stakeholders should meet for an hour or two to document it (using, of course, the project's documented procedure for designing a process).[8] The documentation of the process does not have to be perfect for the DP analysis to be helpful and effective. Once the process is documented, the team is ready to hold a DP workshop.

FIGURE 13-3: Sample Defect Prevention Process

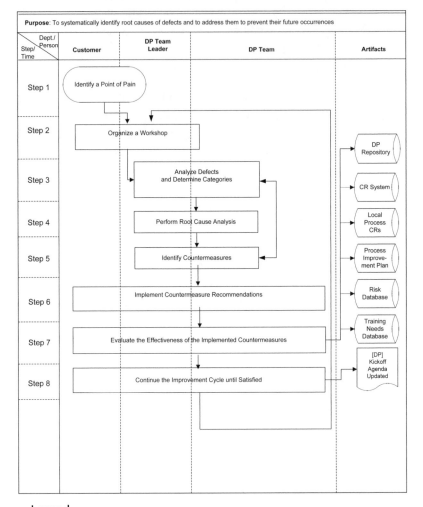

Legend
DP: Defect prevention
CR: Change request

Reproduced by permission from Artech House, Norwood, MA, from *The Requirements Engineering Handbook* by Ralph Young, published 2004.

The objective of a DP workshop is to identify and analyze the defects or problems associated with a process or product. It's best if you have some data and can divide the defects and problems into distinct categories. Even if you don't have data, people who are familiar with the DP process will be able to identify what they believe the major causes of the problems are. Once you have identified the categories of problems, arrange them in descending order; the category that causes the most problems should be listed first. This is called Pareto analysis, and it is a powerful quality improvement technique. Figure 13-4 shows a sample Pareto chart.

The next step is to perform root cause analysis to identify the root causes of the problems or defects. A *root cause* is the underlying reason for a problem. Be sure to look deeper than the symptoms or characteristics of the problem. After you've determined the root causes, you will identify and implement *countermeasures,* actions or steps that eliminate or reduce the root causes of problems.

FIGURE 13-4: Pareto Chart

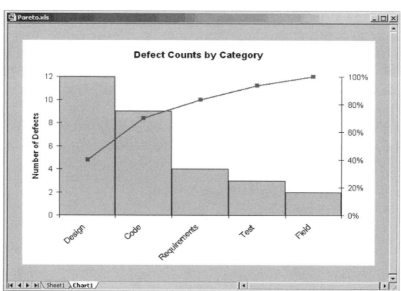

Reproduced by permission from Artech House, Norwood, MA, from *The Requirements Engineering Handbook* by Ralph Young, published 2004.

You will then evaluate the effectiveness of the implemented counter-measures. Don't forget to gather data so that you can back up decisions with facts. After a reasonable period of time, gather the same group of stakeholders that participated in the DP workshop and discuss whether things have improved. Again, it is preferable to have data (you might list data collection as a countermeasure).

Once you've completed the DP process, you will probably want to begin another improvement cycle—that is, you should repeat the entire DP process for the same process or product. Doing so underscores the continuous improvement ethic and habits your team should strive for. Alternatively, the group may decide that it wants to keep the defined countermeasures in place, perhaps making some minor adjustments based on stakeholders' feedback and observations.

The PM should continue to focus on process improvement activities to ensure that they are not only implemented effectively, but also insti-tutionalized. Improvements should become "the way we do business," rather than something that requires a special effort. Process improvement efforts must be nurtured and supported, or they fade away—often much more quickly than they come. Make efforts to reinforce improvements by developing and using checklists and procedures, providing training, tracking results, and providing management sponsorship and support. Management must enthusiastically back process improvements and emphasize their role in helping the project team achieve its goals and objectives. Without the PM's vocal sponsorship and support, any process or quality improvement effort will wane and eventually die.

Quantitative Management

Quantitative management uses statistical process control to identify both common and special causes of variation. This management tech-nique is used for mature projects, which means the project processes have been defined and continuously improved over a period of two to four years. Quantitative management requires people who are experienced in the use of quantitative techniques and who have a detailed understanding of the causes of variation. It can be a powerful tool in support of specific business objectives. For additional information, see Wheeler and Chambers, *Understanding Statistical Process Control.*

Improving Quality by Improving Performance

There has been spectacular progress since the introduction of the personal software process (PSP) in 1997 and the team software process (TSP) in 2000.[9] Achieving these results requires extensive training, discipline, coaching, and leadership, and the use of these techniques is perhaps most appropriate for developing large, real-time programming efforts, as opposed to integrating components that others have written. Before they use TSP, senior developers can hope to achieve about three defects per thousand lines of code (KLOC)—and the numbers are often far worse. TSP teams, however, have delivered an average of 60 defects per million lines of code, according to one study.[10]

In Brief

Managing quality is critical. The PM is responsible, and accountable to all stakeholders, for managing quality. Managing quality necessitates establishing and maintaining a quality culture; using a process-driven approach to perform the project's activities; effectively marshalling and using the skills of an experienced and trained QA manager; managing scope; and performing effective project planning and tracking. In addition, there are four essential mechanisms for building quality into your project: quality control audits, peer reviews and inspections, defect prevention, and quantitative management.

Unfortunately, the approach we've outlined here is rarely used. Most project teams attempt to add quality to work products near the end of the project. The PM must provide the leadership and guidance needed to facilitate a thorough approach to quality.

Suggested Reading and Resources

Grady, Robert, and D. Caswell. *Software Metrics: Establishing a Company-Wide Program.* **Englewood Cliffs, NJ: Prentice Hall, 1987.** This book provides the history, mechanics, and lessons learned of the Hewlett-Packard (HP) company's creation, design, development, and implementation of a successful software metrics program. HP, through its Software Metrics Council, determined to collect size, effort, schedule, and defects data initially. The authors emphasize that PMs reap the greatest benefits from metrics because metrics allow them to better understand project processes and give them measurable indicators of project status.

Grady, Robert. *Practical Software Metrics for Project Management and Process Improvement.* **Englewood Cliffs, NJ: Prentice Hall, 1992.** This second book by Robert Grady extends the concepts and examples of his first book. Grady believes that the SEI CMM can help organizations move toward continuous process improvement, a key to their success.

Humphrey, Watts S. *The Team Software Process (TSP): Coaching Development Teams.* **Boston: Addison-Wesley Professional, 2006.** Most modern software development projects require teamwork, and good teamwork largely determines a project's success. The team software process (TSP), created by Watts S. Humphrey and built upon SEI's Capability Maturity Model® for Software (CMM-SW), is a set of engineering practices and team concepts that can produce effective teams, thereby helping developers deliver high-quality products on time and within budget. Following extensive training, typical first-time TSP teams increase productivity by more than 50 percent and greatly improve the quality of their delivered products. To maintain this improvement, however, TSP teams need the guidance of a capable coach. In this practical guide, Watts provides coaching methods that have repeatedly inspired TSP teams and steered them toward success. Whether you are considering TSP, are actively implementing it, or even if you simply want to understand what is possible, this book provides examples, guidelines, and suggestions you need to get started and grow as a team coach.

Jones, Capers. *Estimating Software Costs.* New York: McGraw Hill, 1998. This book offers a very thorough treatment of its subject. The author worked for IBM and is founder and former chairman of Artemis-Software Productivity Research, Inc. (See www.spr.com.) He has been collecting historical data and designing and building software cost-estimating tools since 1971. His awareness of hundreds of factors that determine the outcome of a project enable him to advise readers on the most critical factors affecting project success.

Paulk, Mark C., Bill Curtis, Mary Beth Chrissis, and Charles V. Weber. *Capability Maturity Model for Software, Version 1.1.* Pittsburgh: Carnegie Mellon University, 1993. The CMM for software (SW-CMM) was the industry framework for software process improvement for more than a decade (1993–2003). It helped projects and organizations evaluate and improve their practices and measure those improvements. This valuable reference is highly recommended for software projects and organizations, though it has been retired by the DOD and the Software Engineering Institute and was superseded by the *Capability Maturity Model Integration for Development (CMMI-DEV), Version 1.2.* Available online at www.sei. cmu.edu.

Quality Assurance Institute (QAI) was founded in 1980 in the United States to provide leadership in quality improvement, productivity, and effective solutions for process management in the information services industry. Its 1,000 corporate members can share state-of-the-art methods, tools, and techniques. QAI offers consulting, education and training services, and assessments. Visit www.QAIworldwide.org.

Rico, David F. *ROI of Software Process Improvement: Metrics for Project Managers and Software Engineers.* Fort Lauderdale, FL: J. Ross Publishing, 2004. This book focuses on software process improvement (SPI) and return on investment (ROI). Rico covers the major SPI approaches (software inspection process, personal and team software processes, CMM and CMMI, and ISO 9001), as well as ROI analysis, benefit analysis, and cost analysis. Visit the publisher's website (www.jrosspub.com/wav) to download invaluable tools, including ROI high-level and detailed models and ISO 9001 and SW-CMM cost models (all in Microsoft Excel format), as well as a supplemental ROI article in Microsoft Word format.

Software Engineering Institute (SEI). *Capability Maturity Model Integration for Development (CMMI-DEV), Version 1.2.* **Pittsburgh: Carnegie Mellon University, 2006.** Although the 1993 *Capability Maturity Model for Software (SW-CMM),* a predecessor of this model, has been retired, it is in our opinion an excellent framework for process improvement for software projects. Another publication, *Systems Engineering CMM (SE-CMM) Version 1.1,* is a great framework for process improvement for systems engineering projects.

The current CMMI covers systems engineering process areas such as technical solutions, product integration, risk management, integrated teaming, and decision analysis and resolution (trade studies). It consists of best practices that address development and maintenance activities throughout the product life cycle, from conception through delivery and maintenance. More recently, the *CMMI for Acquisition, Version 1.2,* and the *CMMI for Services (CMMI-SVC)* have been released.

All these publications are available online at www.sei.cmu.edu.

Wheeler, Donald J., and David S. Chambers. *Understanding Statistical Process Control,* **2nd ed. Knoxville, TN: SPC Press, 1992.** The change from managing projects using good judgment supported by useful metrics to managing projects using quantitative management, and specifically, using statistical process control (SPC), is an amazing transformation. PMs should learn the basic concepts of SPC, and they should ensure someone on staff can apply control charts to the management of project activities. SPC allows PMs to take actions to improve underlying processes. This book, which the authors built upon the works of Walter A. Shewhart and W. Edwards Deming, is about the journey to improve quality, productivity, and project success rates.

Notes

1. Other frameworks you might want to consider, depending on the nature of your project, include the Capability Maturity Model® for Software (SW-CMM), Information Technology Infrastructure Library (ITIL), Personal Software Process (PSP), Team Software Process (TSP), International Standards Organization (ISO) 9000, Control Objectives for Information Technology (COBIT), the Malcolm Baldrige National Quality Program, and the LOGOS Tailored CMM for Small Businesses, Small Organizations, and Small Projects.

2. Karl E. Wiegers, *Peer Reviews in Software: A Practical Guide* (Boston: Addison-Wesley, 2002): 204.

3. Industry expert Capers Jones notes the following about inspections: "It is dismaying to observe the fact that one of the most effective technologies in all of software—[software inspections]—is never used on projects that turn out to be disasters and end up in court. Formal design and code inspections have a 50 year history of successful deployment on large and complex software systems. All 'best in class' software producers utilize software inspections. The measured defect removal efficiency of inspections is more than twice that of most forms of software testing—about 65 percent for inspections versus 30 percent for most kinds of testing. ("Preventing Software Failure: Problems Noted in Breach of Contract Litigation," October 2008, p. 5).

4. This definition of an inspection follows the approach recommended by Tom Gilb and Dorothy Graham in *Software Inspection* (Reading, MA: Addison-Wesley, 1993). Gilb and Graham's approach is quite rigorous. See www.amibug.com for an alternative, less rigorous, and less costly approach.

5. While the SW-CMM has officially been retired by the U.S. Department of Defense and the SEI, it nevertheless provides an invaluable framework for software projects.

6. Technical people are infamous for going off in their own direction, based on their individual experiences and expertise. A lot of time and effort can be saved on a project when the PM actively works to ensure that the project team is working toward the same objectives and that each member of the team feels a responsibility to actively support all other members of the team. The PM needs to articulate these values and to reinforce them constantly.

7. Penny Waugh offers two superb two-hour training sessions, "Peer Review Participant" and "Peer Review Facilitator." In addition, she can provide both these training sessions and also set up project or organization peer review programs, including a peer review notebook that has checklists and procedures in a one-day consulting arrangement. Contact her at waughpenny@aol.com.

8. If your project does not have a documented procedure for designing a

process, you will find a simple, straightforward approach in Ralph R. Young, *The Requirements Engineering Handbook* (Norwood, MA: Artech House, 2004): 180–187.

9. The March 2005 issue of *CrossTalk* is devoted to entirely to the team software process (TSP). That issue is available online at www.stsc.hill. af.mil/crosstalk/2005/03/index.html. Microsoft reports that with their first 200 TSP teams, they invested $3 million and saved $68 million. By using TSP for their tax products, Intuit reduced its 800-number call volume by 800,000 in eight months. Softtek cut turnover by a factor of four, a feat which they credit entirely to their experience using TSP. For a more recent and thorough discussion of achieving improved quality in developed software, see Watts S. Humphrey, "The Software Quality Challenge," in the June 2008 issue of *CrossTalk*, which is available online at www.stsc.hill.af.mil/crosstalk/2008/06/0806Humphrey.html.

10. Noopoor Davis and Julia Mullaney, *The Team Software Process (TSP) in Practice: A Summary of Recent Results*, Technical Report CMU/SEI-2003-TR-014, September 2003.

14 Optimizing the Plan

After spending so much time developing the initial plan, you might think that you should focus only on completing the actual work—that you can't afford to take time to improve the plan. On the contrary, frequently revisiting the plan and updating your project's processes can improve the project's cost-effectiveness, quality, and schedule performance.

On the Software Engineering Institute's (SEI) website, you'll find a presentation (www.sei.cmu.edu/cmmi/presentations/sepg04 .presentations/proof.pdf) by Steve Brady and Sherri Turner from the 2004 SEPG conference. The presentation compares project data from three projects from a single organization. All three projects were of similar size and were executed in similar development environments with similarly skilled employees. But the level of planning and process insertion on the projects varied. Project A did not institute processes, Project B used sound project planning and disciplined processes, and Project C was well planned with strong processes, including processes used throughout the project's life cycle to optimize the plan.

This careful planning and plan optimization substantially and undeniably boosted Project C's bottom line. The project team was able to save more than $148,000 by improving the team's development and code review processes to prevent code defects.

As shown in Figure 14-1, Project C's quality, as represented by defects per thousand lines of code (KLOC), is dramatically higher than that of

FIGURE 14-1: Project Metrics

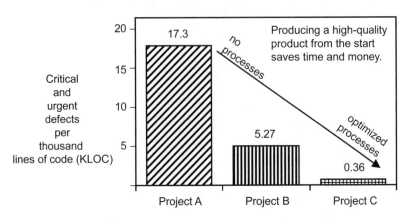

the other two projects. If each of the three projects developed 100,000 lines of code, Project A would have contained 1,700 critical, urgent defects; Project B, 500 critical, urgent defects; and Project C just 36 critical, urgent defects. Consider for a moment how having to remove 1,700 defects, as opposed to 36, would affect your project's cost and schedule. This demonstrates the power of the process that is so often overlooked or underestimated, even by experienced project managers.[1]

Techniques

By building process-improvement techniques into Project C's plan, the team was able to save the project time and money while meeting all of its schedule targets. The team used a combination of statistical process-improvement techniques in conjunction with subjective improvement techniques.

Statistical techniques call for the tracking and use of project metrics. The team used a number of statistical models such as control charts, Rayleigh curves that enable defect prediction (as shown in Figure 14-2), and regression lines to identify and target specific processes in need of improvement, then analyzed changes to those metrics as changes to the project plan were implemented. Using statistics-based decision-making

FIGURE 14-2: Rayleigh Curve

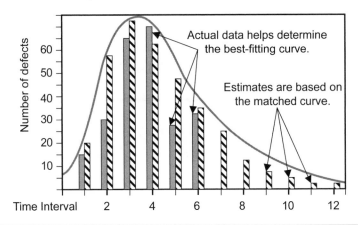

techniques allows the project team to make decisions based on facts rather than feelings. Statistics are one mechanism for tracking and improving the project team's performance. They can tell you which parts of the project are struggling and whether your team's subsequent efforts have made a positive difference.

But not all project improvements are based on data. Statistical methods are a great way to determine whether your project is in control, but the ideas needed to improve processes will come from the people on your team. That's why, when building your plan, you need to use a combination of both statistical and subjective techniques. Subjective techniques call for the project team to use nonstatistical methods to target plan improvement.

Engineering judgment can be a valuable subjective tool for identifying ways to optimize the plan, but you must remember to use engineering judgment in a controlled manner. You don't want to foster an environment in which every team member is exercising engineering judgment; everyone will then do things differently, which leads to a lack of predictability and an undisciplined project approach. To safeguard against the overuse or random use of engineering judgment, you should build "calls" for it into the project plan. For example, the project plan might mandate meetings at the end of each project phase to solicit engineering judgment, defect-prevention cycles at the end of each build, or discussion of process-improvement ideas at scheduled status meetings. (A defect-prevention cycle is an analysis of a specific phase or sub-phase of a project using the same process in an effort to identify and correct the root cause associated with a defect.)

Defect Prevention Using Statistical Methods

In Chapter 7, we discussed using historical data to estimate future work. Recording data is, of course, the key to using it to improve performance. As you analyze the data, you will look for *correlation,* the degree to which two or more data points or groups of data tend to vary together. For example, there is a correlation between baseball hitters' handedness and their performance at bat when facing right-handed or left-handed pitchers. Baseball managers use this correlation to determine which players to start. If a baseball manager knows that the opposing team is starting a right-handed pitcher, he typically stacks his lineup with left-handed hitters in an effort to get more hits.

Development teams are often particularly concerned about product quality. If a team improves the quality of its products, it reduces the time and amount of money that will have to be spent on rework—and boosts customer satisfaction, which is one of the key indicators of business success. Defect density is, then, one of the key metrics for a project to track and improve. Defects can be entered, tracked, and analyzed using a database.

Let's say that we are developing a software application that we have estimated to require more than 100,000 lines of code. Between 300 and 500 lines of code will be examined during each code peer review. As we conducted each peer review, we recorded the number of defects found and put that data into control charts to get an idea of the number of defects we could anticipate finding in future reviews.

From a statistical perspective, *control limits* are established by moving three standard deviations to the left or right of the mean or process average (Figure 14-3). Any data point that falls within these control limits is a data point that one could expect to be produced by the process. Let's say that our team's peer review process had an upper control limit of 38 defects and a lower control limit of eight defects. That means that during any code peer review, you would expect to find between eight and 38 defects. If a peer review shows more than 38 defects, meaning it exceeded the upper control limit, or fewer than eight defects, meaning it fell below the lower control limit, the team would look for a special cause of variation (SCoV) and identify countermeasures to improve the process.

FIGURE 14-3: Special Cause of Variation

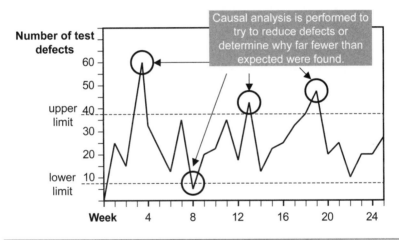

During a peer review of the software code for Project C, we found that the number of defects exceeded the upper control limit. Our SCoV analysis revealed that a developer who usually wrote very good code had written the code being reviewed, but this was the first time he had used Oracle's PL/SQL coding language. Once we realized that the developer's inexperience in PL/SQL was to blame for the high number of defects, we were able to take action. The developer was provided training in PL/SQL and undertook simpler PL/SQL assignments until he had enough experience to take on complex assignments. We were thus able to reduce the number of defects in the code and could spend more time developing new code and less time reworking defective code. Also, we were able to provide a valued team member training that strengthened his skills.

If you use a control chart to track defect density, you might assume that code that breaks the lower control limit must have few or no defects. But it is very unlikely that the code is really *three standard deviations* better than other code being evaluated. The project team should conduct a SCoV to determine the cause of this aberration. It may sound strange to say that you want to *prevent* a zero-defect peer review, but if a review yields no defects, it probably was not done correctly. Possible explanations of the aberration include:

- Peer reviewers may not have been familiar with the language of the code and therefore could not identify defects.

- Peer reviewers, even if skilled, may not have had enough time to thoroughly review the code.

- If checklists were used as part of the review, the checklists the team used may not have covered all possible types of defects.

Defect Prevention Using Nonstatistical Techniques

It's likely that your project team members have years of experience in their fields and much knowledge for you to tap. You can solicit creative ideas from the project team to improve processes and solve project problems.

The development of the software application discussed in Steve Brady and Sherri Turner's 2004 SEPG presentation was split into five builds. Each build was itself a mini-project that yielded a functioning application. To take advantage of the team's creativity and to solicit lessons learned throughout the development process, we scheduled defect-prevention cycles at the end of each build.

We used the defect-prevention cycles to analyze the project team's performance and to get ideas from the team on ways to improve performance for the next build. The sponsor—typically the PM—assigned a defect-prevention cycle lead to conduct the cycle. This lead assembled a team of developers to analyze the defects identified in the completed build. The team searched for common types of defects in the software code and then developed an Ishikawa (fishbone) diagram[2] to help identify the root causes of the defects. After identifying the root causes, the cycle team then developed countermeasures and estimates of how much effort would be needed to implement each countermeasure. The team also estimated how the countermeasures would affect the project. After the team presented its findings to the sponsor, the sponsor worked with the PM to choose which countermeasures to implement.

The team then tracked the project's quality performance in the next build to determine whether the countermeasures actually improved the quality. The SEPG presentation reveals that the project team did improve its performance in each build. After each build, the control limits of subsequent builds tightened, meaning that fewer defects appeared in later builds and that the code development was becoming more and more predictable. This was quantitative evidence that the team's process-improvement ideas were working.

The PM also solicited creative solutions by conducting postmortem meetings at the conclusion of each project phase. To prepare for each of these meetings, the PM collected cost, schedule, and quality data for the phase and asked each team member to come up with at least one improvement idea or to identify at least one lesson learned. At the meeting, the PM presented the cost, schedule, and quality data to the team, and each team member shared his or her process-improvement or lesson-learned idea. To facilitate the exchange of ideas and creative thinking, no one was allowed to interrupt while someone else was speaking. The ideas were documented in the team's meeting minutes by the project's administrative assistant for future reference.

After each team member presented improvement ideas, the team then discussed the ideas presented and how to implement them, identified those that would be most beneficial, selected ideas to execute, and developed action plans to implement the changes.

Keep in mind that change sometimes can't wait until the next defect-prevention cycle or phase postmortem meeting. The team must have a regular forum, such as status meetings, to discuss improvement ideas and challenges. At status meetings for the software development project discussed in the SEPG presentation, team members often raised concerns that had to be addressed long before the next defect-prevention cycle. Sometimes these issues were resolved by the team during the status meeting, but if the issue was too complex to tackle immediately, responsible team members were charged with developing an action plan. Addressing project issues at status meetings allowed us to identify and resolve them before they surfaced in our statistical data. We found that the nonstatistical techniques of project optimization were just as important as the statistical methods.

Return on Investment

Optimizing the plan requires a significant time investment: collecting data, performing defect-prevention cycles, and conducting postmortem meetings are all time-consuming. Time spent optimizing the plan is time not spent developing the product. And team members' time isn't free, so it also costs money for the team to optimize the plan. It's important for PMs to be able to justify this investment of time and money to the project's stakeholders. You will have to show them a return on investment (ROI).

As the 2004 SEPG presentation shows, the Project C team demonstrated to its stakeholders that by investing $11,160 to conduct defect-prevention cycles at the end of each build, it saved $148,500 in developer costs to remove defects. We calculated the savings by assuming that if defects appeared in the code at the same rate for the entire project as they did during the first build, we would have injected 110 more defects. We tracked the time it took to find and repair a defect and multiplied it by the average hourly cost of one of our developers, then multiplied that by a 110-percent overhead rate to obtain the cost to the customer. After the project's stakeholders saw this data, they decided to make the investment in plan optimization.

When optimizing a plan, you should capture defects and make changes as early as you can so that the project benefits from the changes for as long as possible (Figure 14-4). Let's assume that we're working on a software development project that has six phases: requirements, high-level design, detailed design, development, testing, and implementation. We develop the requirements, then take these requirements through the high-level design, detailed design, code development, testing, and implementation phases. When the customer uses the application, the customer identifies a defect that you then trace all the way back to a defective requirement. To correct this defective requirement, you'll have to first fix the requirement in the requirements document, develop the high-level and detailed design, code it, test it, and re-implement it. As you can imagine, the farther back you have to go in the life cycle to repair a defect, the more it will cost you.

Now let's say that we performed a requirements peer review before going on to the high-level design phase and found a defective requirement. We would correct the problem before moving the requirement through

FIGURE 14-4: Defect Prevention

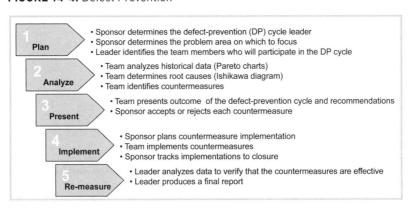

the next phases of the project. When optimizing your plan, the goal is to identify and remove defects in the same phase they are injected. Needless to say, doing this saves a lot of time and money.

If a defect moves from one life cycle phase to the next, it's known as a *phase-escaped defect*. The more phases a defect escapes, the more it will cost the project team to correct the defect. The team will have to trace it back to the point at which it was injected and may have to do a great deal of rework. The rate at which defects escape phases is a key metric to track and reduce. If you minimize phase-escaped defects, you will gain a greater return on investment.

In Brief

The perfect plan does not exist. As the PM, one of your primary responsibilities is to execute your plan while looking for opportunities to improve it. This improvement process is called plan optimization. Implementing lessons learned and incorporating statistical techniques for process improvement, among other tactics, can improve your plan and its effectiveness as well as lower the project's cost and boost quality and schedule performance.

Optimizing the plan requires a significant investment of money and time, so it's very important to be able to justify this investment to the project's stakeholders by demonstrating an ROI. This can be done by carefully tracking the data, analyzing it to determine how plan optimization would benefit the project, and presenting the benefits to stakeholders. One way to increase return on investment is to use peer reviews to identify and remove defects in the same phase during which they are injected.

Suggested Reading and Resources

Neave, Henry R. *The Deming Dimension*. **Knoxville, TN: SPC Press, 1990.** W. Edwards Deming, born in 1900, is often referred to as "the father of quality." Dr. Deming was recognized in the 1980s as a distinguished academic and statistical consultant. In the years after World War II, most

Americans didn't accept his message that management in the Western industrial community smothered the individual, dampened innovation and joy in learning and work, and failed to keep up with quality and competitive position.

This book provides a fundamental understanding of the key concepts of Deming's philosophy, techniques, and recommended management approach. It describes processes, process measurement, key statistical tools and concepts, and their application.

Putnam, Lawrence H. *Measures for Excellence: Reliable Software on Time, Within Budget.* **Englewood Cliffs, NJ: Yourdon Press, 1992.** In this book, the authors emphasize the life cycle model and provide a simple software estimating system. They provide a glossary of more than 100 terms used in quantitative software management, and they explain how conceptual work like software development progresses according to a mathematical curve known as the Rayleigh distribution. This formula helps to understand what happens when you compress a schedule, estimate new projects, and add people to a late project, and it projects the number of defects remaining in a work product.

Software Engineering Institute's Software Engineering Measurement and Analysis (SEMA) website (www.sei.cmu.edu/sema/). This website offers recent publications and training on measurement and analysis. SEI has been interested in measurement and analysis for years and offers a superb training course on this topic.

Notes

1. See Steve McConnell, "The Power of Process," for more evidence of the value of continuous improvement and software development processes. The article is available online at www.stevemcconnell.com/articles/art09. htm.
2. See the Six Sigma Qualtec resource, *QI Story: Tools and Techniques, A Guidebook for Problem Solving,* for concise and helpful information concerning the Ishikawa (fishbone) diagram and many other tools. For more information, visit the Six Sigma Qualtec website at www.ssqi.com.

Final Thoughts
A Recommended Approach for Project Success

This book provides an approach and the tools PMs need to save their projects, and it can also enable PMs to keep future projects from getting into trouble in the first place. A successful project reaches completion on time and within budget, and it meets its goals and objectives. PMs, project team members, and stakeholders can all influence the direction of a project. Using the approaches and tools recommended in this book, PMs will produce high-quality products, minimize rework, accurately predict costs and schedules, satisfy customers, and fulfill staff.

Figure FT-1 provides a high-level or macro process flow chart of the approach recommended in this book. Apply the whole approach to your project or tailor it to your project's particular needs.

It's clear that *all* projects can use some help and support. What would happen if your organization initiated a program to actively assist its projects beginning in their early stages? We know that many organizations are reluctant to establish staff units that contribute to overhead costs. But what if your organization had a project-saving unit that helped project teams develop a project plan; reviewed projects regularly, in each phase of execution; and provided support to help keep them on track? (The project-saving group's manager would need active and vocal top management support for it to succeed.) The group could work toward improvements that might include:

- Development of a comprehensive project plan that is maintained throughout the life of the project.

FIGURE FT-1: The Project-Saving Process

TYPICAL INPUTS	STEPS TO FOLLOW	TYPICAL OUTPUTS
• Business objectives to be met by the project • List of processes that can be re-used • Lessons learned from previous projects	Analyze the Project	• List of necessary new and updated processes • Defined and documented new and updated processes
• Project objectives (specific, achievable) • Requirements plan • Quality management plan • Organizational and project policies	Plan the Plan	• Project plan • Product breakdown structure • Work breakdown structure • Schedule • Budget • List of skills/roles needed and potential candidates • Estimated effort, by role • Project organization chart • Definition of other resources needed • Stakeholders communications plan • Partnering agreement and process • Risk management plan
• Business objectives to be addressed and met by the project • Vision and scope document • Concept of operations (CONOPS) document • Evolved, real, prioritized requirements • Stakeholder expectations	Develop the Plan	
• Project plan • Evolved, real, prioritized requirements • Preliminary design concepts and architecture • Project organization chart • Product breakdown structure • Work breakdown structure • Schedule • Budget • Industry and organizational best practices • Stakeholders communications plan • Team-building activities • Updated list of skills/roles needed and candidates • List of other resources needed • Risk management plan • Senior management sponsorship plan • Proactive communications • Measurement plan • Peer reviews and inspections • Defect prevention • Quality management plan • Project reviews • Acknowledgments and recognitions	Execute the Plan	• Status reports • Configuration and change management • Frequent updates for stakeholders
	Monitor Project Execution	• Planned versus actuals analysis
	Maintain the Plan	• Updated concept of operations (CONOPS) document • New and changed requirements • Updated design concepts and architecture • Project plan • Product breakdown structure • Work breakdown structure • Updated schedule • Updated budget • Actual effort, by role • Project organization chart • Updated list of skills/roles needed and candidates • Updated definition of other resources needed • Updated stakeholders communications plan • Issue resolution actions • Updated risk management plan • Risk register • Project deliverables
	Perform a Project Retrospective (Apply lessons learned to subsequent projects)	

- Development of organizational processes for key process areas.

- An organizational policy that requires all projects to use tailored versions of the organizational processes.

- Creation of an environment of help and support; senior management commits to the concept of assisting projects *before* they get into serious trouble.

- Evolution of a proactive quality management program in the organization, the focus of which is to *help* projects, not to criticize or find fault. This program should include quality management, process improvement, quality assurance, and quality control components.

- Short training courses that are *required* for project staff in all key process areas, institutionalizing a single known method for performing each process area.

- A requirement that all projects initiate and implement a risk management process from project inception and an understanding that PMs are responsible for taking action on identified, prioritized risks.

- A project-leader support mechanism that might include:

  - An e-mail group made up of the organization's PMs that allows them to offer ideas and ask questions.

  - Periodic project-leader workshops in which PMs could share experiences, ideas, useful mechanisms, techniques, tools, and staff with unique capabilities. PMs would take turns leading the workshops.

  - Leadership- and management-development opportunities for PMs. These might include talks by outside motivational speakers, industry or organizational leaders, authors, or representatives of the organization's senior management.

The senior executive typically sponsors this support mechanism by providing vocal and frequent comments to reinforce openness, honesty, quality, leadership, and a focus on processes and continuous improvement.

- A mentoring program for PMs; these programs work well when mentors and mentees are equally committed to their success.

Key Processes and Guidelines

Figure FT-2 provides a summary of the project processes we recommend. These processes are divided into two categories: processes that are executed (implemented) sequentially and processes that are executed throughout the project. An 11" x 17" downloadable version of this figure is available online at www.ralphyoung.net.

Figure FT-3 provides a summary of some of the guidelines for sound project management that we recommend in the book.

Characteristics of the Project Approach We Recommend

We've detailed our strategies for project success in the preceding chapters. In summary, successful projects have much in common. The following elements lay a sturdy foundation for projects that work:

- The PM provides effective leadership and guidance. He or she:

    - Considers him- or herself someone who enables others' success

    - Empowers others to contribute their best efforts

    - Frequently recognizes and appreciates staff

    - Motivates others

    - Fosters powerful teamwork

    - Selects staff thoughtfully and carefully

    - Communicates well and often

    - Fosters meaningful growth of staff; creates and supports personal and professional development.

FIGURE FT-2: Project Management Key Processes

Sequential Processes

Define and agree upon business objectives for the project.
Write a vision and scope document.
Evolve and prioritize real requirements.
Create the team vision.
Initiate the partnering process.
Plan and develop the project plan.
Leverage lessons learned from previous projects.
Execute the plan development process:
- Identify the work products and develop a product breakdown structure.
- Define the work and develop a work breakdown structure.
- Determine the schedule, required skills, and resource plan.
- Determine appropriate quality objectives.

Select the project team.
Perform the development process using inch stones.
Execute the product release authorization process.
Develop a project retrospective.
Leverage lessons learned in future projects.

Continuous Processes

Communicate with stakeholders:
- Manage internal and external stakeholder expectations.
- Conduct project reviews.

Identify and manage risks.
Manage change:
- Control new and changed requirements.
- Conduct configuration management.

Manage quality:
- Peer reviews
- Verification and validation
- Quality control
- Quality assurance
- Quantitative management

Improve processes:
- Defect prevention
- Lessons learned
- Frequent replanning

FIGURE FT-3: Guidelines for Sound Project Management

1. Develop and maintain a realistic project plan to ensure project success. Replan regularly.
2. Manage internal and external stakeholder expectations.
3. Evolve all real requirements before beginning other technical work.
4. Once the development process has begun, manage new and changed requirements closely. Failing to do this often leads to requirements creep, which is likely to jeopardize the development effort.
5. Develop and use a product breakdown structure, work breakdown structure, and schedule, and determine appropriate quality objectives—these are integral components of the plan development process.
6. Identify all the required products and work upfront, to avoid putting the project behind schedule and over budget from the start.
7. Write a vision and scope document to facilitate a successful project launch or to help save a troubled project already in progress.
8. Establish trust and foster effective teamwork through the partnering process. This is essential for project success.
9. Be able to articulate what quality means on your project, create a quality culture, build quality into work products, execute an effective product release authorization process, and use peer reviews, quality assurance, quality control, configuration management, and risk identification and management effectively.
10. Develop, use, and continuously improve project processes to ensure consistency, fewer defects, lower costs, improved schedules, high-quality work products, and customer satisfaction.
11. Work hard to identify and implement proactive steps to foster effective communications.
12. Take advantage of actual data—both from your own projects and from other projects—to estimate the costs and work required to perform future project activities.
13. Document your estimation approaches; compare estimates with actuals; and work to continuously improve your estimation process.
14. Recognize and appreciate good work and celebrate project milestones.
15. Be an effective leader—one who continues to grow throughout his or her career. To this end, consider creating a personal development plan. Dedicated PMs should always make time in their busy schedules for professional development.

- The project uses proven, effective requirements practices. The requirements for the project have been evolved from stated requirements into real requirements through a collaborative effort involving leaders from all stakeholder groups. The PM has invested 8 to 14 percent of total project costs in the project's requirements process, including effective mechanisms to control new requirements and changes to requirements and to deliver products in a way that accommodates inevitable change.

- The project team develops and uses a product breakdown structure (PBS) that identifies all of the required work products. The work estimation process is continually refined, and the team uses standard templates, procedures, and checklists to build the PBS and to perform the actual work. Quality standards are identified and used.

- The project team develops and uses a WBS, which identifies all the required work.

- The project team develops and uses a schedule.

- The project team develops and uses a process-based approach. Defined, documented, and continuously improved processes are used to perform the project's work activities.

- An effective risk management process is used from the beginning of the project.

- An attitude, habit, and culture of continuous improvement are fostered and permeate the team's work.

- Quality is built into the work products. To ensure quality, the team employs:

  ◆ Early peer reviews and inspections of work products

  ◆ Trained peer reviewers and peer review facilitators

  ◆ A defect prevention (DP) process and repeated DP cycles to fix root causes of problems by identifying and deploying effective countermeasures.

- Quality is valued by all stakeholders. The team engages in quality assurance, quality management, and quality control processes.

- The team relies on leading indicators to guide management actions; management takes effective action promptly.

It is often said that project failure starts within the first 20 percent of a project. Getting off to a solid start and adjusting the plan accordingly as problems crop up are critical to the success of any project. Our hope is that you will develop a project plan and apply the practical tools and techniques needed to execute it. If your project hasn't yet begun, applying these techniques should prevent a few missteps; if your project is already in trouble, we believe we have equipped you with what you need to turn it around. Remember, your work won't be perfect the first time out, and that's okay. The truth is that none of us will ever be perfect. But if you keep working to get better, you'll find you can get pretty darn close.

Suggested Reading and Resources

Kendrick, Tom. *The Project Management Tool Kit: 100 Tips and Techniques for Getting the Job Done Right.* New York: American Management Association, 2004. This book provides concise explanations of useful project management tools and techniques, including:

- Resolving conflicts

- Building consensus

- Estimating costs

- Delegating responsibility

- Assessing lessons learned

- Negotiating contracts

- Writing a project charter

- Setting project priorities

- Ensuring quality control

- Leveling resources

- Analyzing returns on investment

- Offering rewards and recognition

- Using software tools to manage projects

McConnell, Steve. *Professional Software Development: Shorter Schedules, Higher Quality Products, More Successful Projects, Enhanced Careers.* **Boston: Addison-Wesley, 2004.** In this book, McConnell expands on the themes he presented in his previous book, *After the Gold Rush,* by encouraging software engineers to become better professionals all around. The book's companion website, www.construx.com, contains professional reading lists, self-study plans, descriptions of current certification and licensing initiatives, links to software engineering programs, and pointers to many related websites. He addresses individual, organizational, and industry professionalism.

Acronyms

BPM	Build Process Model
PBEV	Performance-Based Earned Value
CAR	Causal Analysis and Resolution
CM	Configuration Management
CMM-SW	Capability Maturity Model® for Software
CMMI	Capability Maturity Model® Integration
COCOMO	Constructive Cost Model
COTS	Commercial Off-the-Shelf
DACS	Data and Analysis Center for Software
DOD	Department of Defense
DOS	Disk Operating System
DP	Defect Prevention
DSB	Defense Science Board
EIA	Electronics Industries Alliance
ERA	Earned Run Average
EV	Earned Value
GPS	Global Positioning System
INCOSE	International Council on Systems Engineering
KLOC	Thousand Lines of Code
KPA	Key Process Area

NDIA	National Defense Industry Association
NASA	National Aeronautics and Space Administration
PBS	Product Breakdown Structure
PDCA	Plan, Do, Check, Act
PDP	Plan Development Process
PL/SQL	Programming Language for SQL
PM	Project Manager
PMBOK®	Project Management Body of Knowledge
PMI	Project Management Institute
PRA	Product Release Authorization
PSP	Personal Software Process
QA	Quality Assurance
QC	Quality Control
QI	Quality Improvement
QIT	Quality Improvement Team
QM	Quality Management
QM	Quantitative Management
RA	Requirements Analyst
RFP	Request for Proposal
ROI	Return on Investment
RTM	Requirements Traceability Matrix
SEI	Software Engineering Institute
SEPG	Software and Systems Engineering Process Group
SCOV	Special Cause of Variation
SOW	Statement of Work
SPMN	Software Program Managers Network
SPC	Statistical Process Control
SQL	Structure Query Language
WBS	Work Breakdown Structure

Glossary

Artifact: A written document, often a work product (e.g., a documented plan, a checklist).

Brainstorming: A group problem-solving technique involving spontaneous contributions of ideas from all members of the group, to encourage creative thinking and generate ideas quickly.

Build process model (BPM): Describes the high-level processes that the team will use to execute the project.

Control chart: A line graph specifically used to track the trend or performance of a process over time. This is accomplished by observing how the variability within the process causes the trend line to fluctuate within a pair of statistically calculated limits. Control charts illustrate process variability.

Correlation: The degree to which two or more data points or groups tend to vary together.

Countermeasures: Actions or steps that eliminate or reduce the root causes of problems.

Customer: The person or organization that pays for a project or its end products. The customer is not necessarily the user.

Defect prevention (DP): Using technologies, techniques (e.g., peer reviews), and methodologies (e.g., six sigma, joint application design, structured design) that reduce the risk of making errors in deliverables.

Defect prevention (DP) cycle: An analysis of a specific project phase or sub-phase in an effort to identify and correct the root cause associated with a defect.

Defect removal: Refers to all activities used to find errors or deficiencies in any kind of deliverable (e.g., requirements inspections, design inspections, document inspections, code inspections, automated static analysis of code, complexity analysis, testing).

Defect removal efficiency: The percentage of defects discovered before the product is delivered to clients or users. For example, if the development team finds 900 defects and addresses them, and then subsequently users find 100 defects within a standard period of time after the product release—usually 90 days—then the defect removal efficiency is 90 percent.

Deliverables: Work products that are delivered to the customer.

Dependency: An event or activity that must occur in order for something else to occur. For example, project members and stakeholders must understand the project vision and scope before they can define and document real requirements.

Functionality: The quality of being able to perform a particular task.

Inch stone: A small unit of work whose duration is measured in hours. Breaking project work into inch stones allows the team to quickly ascertain progress or lack thereof.

Inspection: A rigorous form of peer review, in which the project team, PM, and perhaps other interested and significant parties review the project in meticulous detail to determine whether it meets the requirements.

Interfaces: Related systems with which an effort must interact.

Lagging indicators: Metrics that provide information about events that have already occurred.

Leading indicators: Metrics that provide insight into potential problems.

Mechanism: A way to get something done or achieve a result.

Milestone: A specific project event that occurs at a specific point in time. Classifying milestones as such gives the event priority and significance.

Mindset: Mental inclination, tendency, or habit.

Multivoting: A structured series of votes that a team uses to help reduce a large number of items to a manageable few—usually three to five. Multivoting helps reduce lists quickly and with a high degree of consensus.

Negative stakeholder: Someone who is not an advocate for the project or who actively works against the project's objectives.

Partnering process: A structured process designed to create an atmosphere of commitment, cooperation, and collegial problem solving among organizations and individuals working together on a project. Partnering uses mutually developed vision statements, common goals, guiding principles, issue-resolution procedures, and evaluation methods to help ensure project success. The process is normally initiated during a workshop at the beginning of a project.

Peer review: An activity in which one or more persons who are not the author or creator of a work product examine that product with the intent of finding defects and improvement opportunities.

Phase-escaped defect: A defect that is not identified and removed in the same phase in which it first occurred.

Plan development process (PDP): The process you'll go through to develop the plan and all of its components. The PDP is typically led by the project manager, with participation from team leads, and can include any members of the project team on staff at the time. As new team members are hired, they should be included in the PDP process as well, until the plan is complete.

Plan optimization: Identifying and implementing opportunities to improve a plan.

Process maturity level: The degree to which processes are used, defined, documented, and understood.

Process owner: An individual selected by an organization or a project to serve as an advocate for a particular process area (e.g., project planning, quality assurance, configuration management). The process owner should be knowledgeable and provide advice, information, and assistance in applying the process to the project.

Product: Any tangible item that will be produced as a result of conducting a project.

Product breakdown structure (PBS): A tool developed by a project planning team to identify and capture all of the products the project will create, their respective sizes, and quality requirements.

Project: An undertaking focused on developing or maintaining one or more products. Typically, a project has its own funding, accounting, and delivery schedule.

Project capability: A project's ability to meet its objectives.

Project champion: An advocate for the project who is very familiar with customer needs and who plays an active and vocal role in the development effort, facilitating the tasks of the development team. The project champion defends the project, for example, to the project sponsor and to critics of the project.

Project sponsor: The person or organization that provides funding for a project.

Quality: The fulfillment of real customer needs.

Quality assurance (QA): A process in which policies, processes, and work results are independently evaluated and management is given feedback.

Quality control: Mechanisms that ensure work products meet specified criteria.

Quality culture: The presence of an attitude of continuous improvement and customer satisfaction in a project or an organization.

Quality management: Integrating practices to build continuous improvement into a work approach.

Quantitative management: Management strategy that bases decisions on data.

Quantitative report: Describes the percentage of completed work relative to the work planned for completion at that point in the schedule.

Real requirements: The subset of the stated requirements that reflects the verified and prioritized needs for a particular system or capability.

Requirements analysis: A structured method used to examine the attributes that will satisfy a customer need.

Requirements churn: A lack of clarity over requirements that results in agitation and confusion during the development effort.

Requirements creep: Changes to requirements or new requirements added without any control or management after the initial set of requirements is defined.

Requirements elicitation: The process of emerging the real requirements from user needs and the stated requirements.

Resource loading: The process of assigning resources to tasks provided in the schedule.

Root cause: The underlying reason for a problem; the major stimulus behind an undesired condition.

Sampling: The process of selecting a representative part of a population to determine characteristics of the entire population.

Scaled: An item that is reduced or increased in size and scope as required for a particular function.

Schedule: A component of a plan that indicates the intended time and sequence of needed tasks.

Scope creep: The acceptance of new requirements and changes to requirements without any control or management.

Special cause of variation (SCoV): A statistical process that identifies an activity that is considered outside the norm—i.e., something reflecting a new, unanticipated, emergent, or previously neglected phenomenon within a system. If detected, its root cause is determined and countermeasures are identified to prevent this abnormal activity from reoccurring.

Stakeholder: Anyone who has an interest in the success or failure of a project.

Stated requirements: The requirements provided by a customer at the beginning of a development effort.

Successful project: An effort that is finished within the currently identified budget and schedule and that meets its established goals and objectives.

Tailored: An item that is changed to fulfill a particular need, application, or project.

Trade study: An analysis of alternative courses of action. Trade studies can be used to identify the best approach or alternative for a particular project or system.

User: An individual or group that uses a product or system.

Work breakdown structure (WBS): A tool developed by a project planning team to identify all the work required to complete the project and its estimated duration. The documented work activities are linked to the products listed in the product breakdown structure (PBS).

References

ABT Corporation. "Core Competencies for Project Managers." White Paper, 2000. Available online at www.tsepm.com/may00/art.5.htm.

Alexander, Ian F., and Richard Stevens. *Writing Better Requirements.* London: Addison-Wesley, 2002.

Alexander, Ian F., and Neil Maiden. *Scenarios, Stories, Use Cases: through the Systems Development Life-Cycle.* West Sussex, England: John Wiley & Sons, 2004.

Alexander, Ian F., and Ljevka Bens-Dvorkic. *Discovering Requirements.* Hoboken, NJ: John Wiley & Sons, 2009.

Bennis, Warren, and Patricia Ward Biederman. *Genius: The Secrets of Creative Collaboration.* Reading, MA: Perseus Books, 1997.

Boehm, Barry W. *Software Engineering Economics.* Englewood Cliffs, NJ: Prentice Hall, 1981.

Boehm, Barry W., Chris Abts, A. Winsor Brown, Sunita Chulani, Bradford K. Clark, Ellis Horowitz, Ray Madachy, Donald J. Reifer, and Bert Steece. *Software Cost Estimation with COCOMO II.* Reading, MA: Addison-Wesley, 2000.

Broadman, Judith G., and Donna L. Johnson. *The LOGOS Tailored CMM for Small Businesses, Small Organizations, and Small Projects.* Needham, MA: LOGOS International, Inc., 1996. Available online at www.logos-intl.com.

Brooks, Jr., Frederick P. *The Mythical Man-Month: Essays on Software Engineering.* Reading, MA: Addison-Wesley, 1995.

Brooks, Jr., Frederick P. *The Design of Design: Essays from a Computer Scientist.* Boston, MA: Addison-Wesley, 2009.

Brown, Norm. "Industrial-Strength Management Strategies." *IEEE Software* 13.4 (July 1996): 94–103.

Burlton, Roger T. *Business Process Management: Profiting from Process.* Indianapolis, ID: Sams Publishing, 2001.

Cagle, Ronald B. *Blueprint for Project Recovery: The Complete Process for Getting Derailed Projects Back on Track.* New York: AMACOM, 2003.

Carr, Frank, with Kim Hurtado, Charles Lancaster, Charles Markert, and Paul Tucker. *Partnering in Construction: A Practical Guide to Project Success.* Chicago, IL: American Bar Association Publishing, 1999.

Capability Maturity Model® Integration. See www.sei.cmu.edu/cmmi.

Cole, Peter S. *How to Write a Statement of Work*, 5th ed. Vienna, VA: Management Concepts, 2003.

Constructive Cost Model II (COCOMO II). See http://sunset.usc.edu/csse/research/COCOMOII/cocomo_main.html.

Covey, Stephen R. *The 8th Habit: From Effectiveness to Greatness.* New York: Free Press, 2004.

Data and Analysis Center for Software (DACS) Gold Practices. See www.goldpractices.com/practices.

Defense Science Board (DSB). *Report of the Defense Science Board (DSB) Task Force on Defense Software.* Washington, D.C.: Department of Defense, 2000. Available online at www.acq.osd.mil/dsb/reports/defensesoftware.pdf.

DeMarco, Tom, and Timothy Lister. *Peopleware: Productive Projects and Teams*, 2nd ed. New York: Dorset House Publishing Company, 1999.

Doyle, Michael, and David Straus. *How to Make Meetings Work.* Berkeley Publishing, 1993.

Electronic Industries Alliance (EIA). *ANSI/EIA 632, Processes for Engineering a System.* Arlington, VA: EIA, 1998.

Gaffney, Steven. *Just Be Honest: Authentic Communication Strategies That Get Results and Last a Lifetime.* Arlington, VA: JMG Publishing, 2002.

Gilb, Tom. For information about impact estimation, see www.gilb.com.

Gilb, Tom, and Dorothy Graham. *Software Inspection.* Reading, MA: Addison-Wesley, 1993.

Goldratt, Eliyahu M., *Critical Chain.* Great Berrington, MA: The North River Press, 1997.

Goldratt, Eliyahu M. and Jeff Cox. *The Goal,* 2nd ed. Great Berrington, MA: The North River Press, 1992.

Gottesdiener, Ellen. *Requirements by Collaboration: Workshops for Defining Needs.* Reading, MA: Addison-Wesley, 2002.

Grady, Robert. *Practical Software Metrics for Project Management and Process Improvement.* Englewood Cliffs, NJ: Prentice Hall, 1992.

Grady, Robert, and D. Caswell. *Software Metrics: Establishing a Company-Wide Program.* Englewood Cliffs, NJ: Prentice Hall, 1987.

Hadden, Rita Chao. *Leading Culture Change in Your Software Organization: Delivering Results Early.* Vienna, VA: Management Concepts, 2003.

Haugan, Gregory T. *Work Breakdown Structures for Projects, Programs, and Enterprises.* Vienna, VA: Management Concepts, 2008.

Hooks, Ivy F. "Guide for Managing and Writing Requirements." 1994. Available by email from ivy@complianceautomation.com.

Hooks, Ivy F. "Managing Requirements." Available online at www.complianceautomation.com.

Hooks, Ivy F. "Writing Good Requirements." This one-day tutorial is available online at www.incose.org.uk/incose99/tuts.htm.

Hooks, Ivy F., and Kristin A. Farry. *Customer-Centered Products: Creating Successful Products through Smart Requirements Management.* New York: AMACOM, 2001.

Horine, Greg. *Absolute Beginner's Guide to Project Management*, 2nd ed. Indianapolis: Pearson Education, 2009.

Hossenlopp, Rosemary, and Kathleen B. Hass. *Unearthing Business Requirements: Elicitation Tools and Techniques.* Vienna, VA: Management Concepts, 2008.

Humphrey, Watts S. "The Software Quality Challenge." *CrossTalk: The Journal of Defense Software Engineering.* Hill Air Force Base, UT: The Software Technology Support Center, June 2008. Available online at www.stsc.hill.af.mil/crosstalk/2008/06/0806Humphrey.html.

Humphrey, Watts S. "The Process Revolution." *CrossTalk: The Journal of Defense Software Engineering.* Hill Air Force Base, UT: The Software Technology Support Center, August 2008. Available online at www.stsc.hill.af.mil/crosstalk/2008/08/0808Humphrey.html.

Humphrey, Watts S. *Winning with Software: An Executive Strategy.* Reading, MA: Addison-Wesley, 2002.

Humphrey, Watts S. *Introduction to the Team Software Process.* Reading, MA: Addison-Wesley, 2000.

Humphrey, Watts S. "Why Don't They Practice What We Preach?" *Annals of Software Engineering* 6.1–4 (1998): 201–222.

Humphrey, Watts S. *Introduction to the Personal Software Process.* Reading, MA: Addison-Wesley, 1997.

Humphrey, Watts S. *Managing Technical People: Innovation, Teamwork, and the Software Process.* Reading, MA: Addison-Wesley, 1997.

Jones, Capers. *Assessment and Control of Software Risks.* Englewood Cliffs, NY: Yourdon Press, 1994.

Jones, Capers. *Estimating Software Costs.* McGraw Hill, 1998.

Jones, Capers. "Software Project Management Practices: Failure Versus Success." *CrossTalk: The Journal of Defense Software Engineering* 17 (October 2004): 5–9.

Jones, Capers. "Measuring Defect Potential and Defect Removal Efficiency®." *CrossTalk: The Journal of Defense Software Engineering.* Hill Air Force Base, UT: The Software Technology Support Center, June 2008. Available online at www.stsc.hill.af.mil/crosstalk/2008/06/0806Jones.html.

Jones, Capers. "Preventing Software Failure: Problems Noted in Breach of Contract Litigation." October 2008. See www.SPR.com.

Kendrick, Tom. *The Project Management Tool Kit: 100 Tips and Techniques for Getting the Job Done Right.* New York: American Management Association, 2004.

Kerth, Norman L. *Project Retrospectives: A Handbook for Team Reviews.* New York: Dorset House Publishing, 2001.

Kharbanda, Om Prakash, and Jeffery K. Pinto. *What Made Gertie Gallop: Learning from Project Failures.* New York: Von Nostrand Reinhold Company, 1996.

Kouzes, James M., and Barry Z. Posner. *The Leadership Challenge,* 4th ed. Hoboken, NJ: John Wiley & Sons, 2007.

Lauesen, Soren. *Software Requirements: Styles and Techniques.* Reading, MA: Addison-Wesley, 2002.

Leffingwell, Dean, and Don Widrig. *Managing Software Requirements: A Unified Approach.* Reading, MA: Addison-Wesley, 2000.

Markert, Charles. *Partnering: Unleashing the Power of Teamwork.* This presentation is available by email from markert@erols.com.

Martin, Paula, and Karen G. Tate. *Project Management Memory Jogger™: A Pocket Guide for Project Teams.* Salem, NH: GOAL/QPC, 1997.

McConnell, Steve. *Software Estimation: Demystifying the Black Art.* Redmond, WA: Microsoft Press, 2006.

McConnell, Steve. *Professional Software Development: Shorter Schedules, Higher Quality Products, More Successful Projects, Enhanced Careers.* Boston: Addison-Wesley, 2004.

McConnell, Steve. *Software Project Survival Guide*. Redmond, WA: Microsoft Press, 1998.

McConnell, Steve. *Rapid Development: Taming Wild Software Schedules*. Redmond, WA: Microsoft Press, 1996.

McConnell, Steve. "The Power of Process." *Computer* 31 (May 1998). Available online at www.stevemcconnell.com/articles/art09.htm.

McDonald, Marc, Robert Musson, and Ross Smith. *The Practical Guide to Defect Prevention*. Redmond, WA: Microsoft Press, 2008.

Neave, Henry R. *The Deming Dimension*. Knoxville, TN: SPC Press, 1990.

O'Connell, Fergus. *How to Run Successful Projects II*, 2nd ed. New York: Prentice Hall, 1996.

Pacelli, Lonnie. *The Project Management Advisor: 18 Major Screw-ups, and How to Cut Them Off at the Pass*. Upper Saddle River, NJ: Prentice Hall, 2004.

Paulk, Mark C. "The Soft Side of Software Process Improvement." Pittsburgh, PA: Software Engineering Institute, 1999.

Paulk, Mark C., Bill Curtis, Mary Beth Chrissis, and Charles V. Weber. *Capability Maturity Model for Software, Version 1.1*. Pittsburgh, PA: Software Engineering Institute, 1993. Available online at www.sei.cmu.edu/publications/documents/93.reports/93.tr.024.html.

Paulk, Mark C., Charles V. Weber, Suzanne M. Garcia, Mary Beth Chrissis, and Marilyn W. Bush. *Key Practices of the Capability Maturity Model, Version 1.1*. Pittsburgh, PA: Software Engineering Institute, 1993.

Porter-Roth, Bud. *Request for Proposal: A Guide to Effective RFP Development*. Reading, MA: Addison-Wesley, 2002.

Powell, Robert A., and Dennis M. Buede. *The Project Manager's Guide to Making Successful Decisions*. Vienna, VA: Management Concepts, 2009.

Project Management Institute. *Guide to the Project Management Body of Knowledge (PMBOK® Guide)*, 3rd ed. Newtown Square, PA: Project Management Institute, 2004.

Purba, Sanjiv, and Joseph J. Zucchero. *Project Rescue: Avoiding a Project Management Disaster.* New York: Osborne McGraw-Hill, 2004.

Putnam, Lawrence H. *Measures for Excellence: Reliable Software On Time, Within Budget.* Englewood Cliffs, NJ: Yourdon Press, 1992.

Quality Assurance Institute (QAI). See www.QAIworldwide.org.

Rico, David F. *ROI of Software Process Improvement: Metrics for Project Managers and Software Engineers.* Fort Lauderdale, FL: J. Ross Publishing, 2004.

Rothman, Johanna. "How to Use Inch-Pebbles When You Think You Can't." Rothman Consulting Group, Inc., 1999. Online at www .jrothman.com/Papers/Howinch-pebbles.html.

Russell, Lou, and Jeff Feldman. *IT Leadership Alchemy.* Upper Saddle River, NJ: Prentice Hall PTR, 2003.

Sabourin, Rob. Software development project resources. See www .amibug.com.

Scholtes, Peter R., Brian L. Joiner, and Barbara J. Streibel. *The Team Handbook*, 2nd ed. Madison, WI: Oriel, 2001.

Sheard, Sarah. "What Is Senior Management Commitment?" Updated from International Council on Systems Engineering Symposium Proceedings, 2001. Systems and Software Consortium, Inc., 2001. To request a copy, please contact Ms. Sheard at sheard@ systemsandsoftware.org.

Six Sigma Qualtec. *QI Story: Tools and Techniques, A Guidebook to Problem Solving*, 3rd ed. Tempe, AZ: Six Sigma Qualtec, 1999.

Software Engineering Institute. *Capability Maturity Model Integration for Development (CMMI-DEV), Version 1.2.* Pittsburgh, PA: Software Engineering Institute, 2006. Available online at www.sei.cmu.edu/ publications/documents/06.reports/06tr008.html.

Software Engineering Institute. *Capability Maturity Model Integration for Services (CMMI-SVC), Version 1.0.* Pittsburgh, PA: Software Engineering Institute, 2009.

Software Engineering Institute's Software Engineering Measurement and Analysis (SEMA). See www.sei.cmu.edu/sema.

Solomon, Paul J., and Ralph R. Young. *Performance-Based Earned Value.* Hoboken, NJ: John Wiley & Sons, 2007.

Stevens, Richard, Peter Brook, Ken Jackson, and Stuart Arnold. *Systems Engineering: Coping with Complexity.* London: Prentice Hall Europe, 1998.

"Team Software Process." *CrossTalk: The Journal of Defense Software Engineering.* Hill Air Force Base, UT: The Software Technology Support Center, March 2005. Available online at www.stsc.hill. af.mil/crosstalk/2005/03/index.html.

Tsui, Frank. *Managing Software Projects.* Sudbury, MA: Jones and Bartlett Publishers, 2004.

Walton, Mary. *The Deming Management Method.* New York: The Putnam Publishing Group, 1986.

Weinberg, Gerald. *Becoming a Technical Leader: An Organic Problem-Solving Approach.* New York: Dorset House, 1986.

Weller, Ed. "Practical Applications of Statistical Process Control." *Proceedings of the 10th International Conference on Software Quality,* July 2000.

Wheeler, Donald J., and David S. Chambers. *Understanding Statistical Process Control,* 2nd ed. Knoxville, TN: SPC Press, 1992.

White, Cheryl L. *Change on Demand: The Science of Turbo Charging Change in the Millennium.* Portland, OR: Eddlesen & Rowe LLC, 2000.

Whitten, Neal. *Neal Whitten's Let's Talk! More No-Nonsense Advice for Project Success.* Vienna, VA: Management Concepts, 2007.

Whitten, Neal. *Neal Whitten's No-Nonsense Advice for Successful Projects.* Vienna, VA: Management Concepts, 2005.

Wiegers, Karl E. *Practical Project Initiation*. Redmond, WA: Microsoft Press, 2007.

Wiegers, Karl E. "See You In Court." *Software Development Magazine* 11.1 (January 2003). Available online at www.processimpact.com.

Wiegers, Karl E. *Peer Reviews in Software: A Practical Guide*. Boston: Addison-Wesley, 2002.

Wiegers, Karl E. "Habits of Effective Analysts." *Software Development Magazine* 8.10 (October 2000): 62–65.

Wiegers, Karl E. "Stop Promising Miracles." *Software Development Magazine* (February 2000). Available online at www.ddj.com/dept/architect/184414570.

Wiegers, Karl E. *Creating a Software Engineering Culture*. New York: Dorset House, 1996.

Young, Ralph R. *Effective Requirements Practices*. Boston: Addison-Wesley, 2001.

Young, Ralph R. *Project Requirements: A Guide to Best Practices*. Vienna, VA: Management Concepts, 2006.

Young, Ralph R. "Twelve Requirements Basics for Project Success." *CrossTalk: The Journal of Defense Software Engineering*. Hill Air Force Base, UT: The Software Technology Support Center, December 2006. Available online at www.stsc.hill.af.mil/crosstalk/2006/12/0612Young.html.

Young, Ralph R. *The Requirements Engineering Handbook*. Boston: Artech House, 2004.

Young, Ralph R. "Recommended Requirements Gathering Practices." *CrossTalk: The Journal of Defense Software Engineering*. Hill Air Force Base, UT: The Software Technology Support Center, April 2002. Available online at www.stsc.hill.af.mil/crosstalk/2002/04/young.html.

Index

The 77 Deadly Sins of Project Management
Management Concepts

Projects can be negatively impacted by common "sins" that hinder, stall, or throw the project off track. *The 77 Sins of Project Management* helps you better understand how to execute projects by providing individual anecdotes and case studies of the project management sins described by experts in the field.

ISBN 978-1-56726-246-9 ■ Product Code B469 ■ approx. 250 pages

Work Breakdown Structures for Projects, Programs, and Enterprises
Gregory T. Haugan, Ph.D., PMP

The basic concept and use of the work breakdown structure (WBS) are fundamental in project management. In *Work Breakdown Structures for Projects, Programs, and Enterprises*, author Gregory T. Haugan, originator of the widely accepted 100 percent rule, offers an expanded understanding of the WBS concept, illustrating its principles and applications for planning programs as well as its use as an organizing framework at the enterprise level. Through specific examples, this book will help you understand how the WBS aids in the planning and management of all functional areas of project management.

ISBN 978-1-56726-228-5 ■ Product Code B285 ■ 382 pages

Managing Politics and Conflict in Projects
Brian Irwin, PMP

Managing Politics and Conflict in Projects is an easy-to-read, no-nonsense guide that walks you through the "soft" issues of project management, including communicating, negotiating, and influencing skills that are vital to your project success. Understand your organization's political climate and culture and ascend the corporate ladder to the next level as a project manager. Learn how to deal with political issues requiring complex organizational and interpersonal skills, using valuable review points, tips, and a fictional narrative illustrating the book's main points.

ISBN 978-1-56726-221-6 ■ Product Code B216 ■ 213 pages

Project Decisions: The Art and Science
Lev Virine and Michael Trumper

Project management is the art of making the right decisions. To be effective as a project manager, you must be aware of how to make rational choices in project management, what processes can help you to improve these choices, and what tools are available to help you through this process. *Project Decisions: The Art and Science* is an easy-to-read practical guide to the project decision analysis process. This valuable text presents the basics of cogitative psychology and quantitative analysis methods to help project managers make better decisions.

ISBN 978-1-56726-217-9 ■ Product Code B179 ■ 344 pages